A CHRISTIAN'S SURVIVAL GUIDE

RICHARD MAYHUE

While this book is intended for the reader's personal enjoyment and profit, it is also intended for group study. A Leader's Guide with Victor Multiuse Transparency Masters is available from your local bookstore or from the publisher.

VICTOR BOOKS
A DIVISION OF SCRIPTURE PRESS PUBLICATIONS INC.
USA CANADA ENGLAND

Scripture quotations are from the *New American Standard Bible,* © the Lockman Foundation 1960, 1962, 1963, 1968, 1971, 1972, 1973, 1975, 1977.

Recommended Dewey Decimal Classification: 221.92

Suggested Subject Heading: BIBLE—BIOGRAPHY

Library of Congress Catalog Card Number: 86-63155

ISBN: 0-89693-720-8

© 1987 by SP Publications, Inc. All rights reserved. Printed in the United States of America. No part of this book may be used or reproduced in any manner whatsoever without written permission except in the case of brief excerpts in books, critical articles, and reviews. For information address Victor Books, P.O. Box 1825, Wheaton, Illinois 60189.

CONTENTS

Foreword 5
Introduction 7

I. WARNING—SOME FAILED TO WIN
1. *Solomon: The Shipwrecked Saint* 13
2. *Jonah: The Wrong-Way Prophet* 26
3. *Eve: A Long-Shot Loser* 36
4. *Saul: The "My Way" Monarch* 48

II. HOPE—SOME FELL BUT RECOVERED WHILE FIGHTING
5. *Elijah: The Lone Prophet* 61
6. *Samson: The Wayward Warrior* 73
7. *Habakkuk: God's Man from Missouri* 84
8. *Moses: A Successful Failure* 94

III. ENCOURAGEMENT—SOME FOUGHT TO VICTORY
9. *Joseph: God's Valedictorian* 107
10. *Job: A Righteous Victor* 120
11. *Ruth: God's Cinderella* 132
12. *Daniel: A Man of High Esteem* 142

Notes 153

To the
elders, staff, and flock at
Grace Brethren Church of Long Beach,
beloved fellow-soldiers
with whom I share the battle of life.

FOREWORD

ACCORDING TO SCRIPTURE, true Christian education should be centered on teaching moral and godly character first, and knowledge second. The reason is very simple. *What you are is more important than what you know.* This great truth has been lost by most modern educators in the public arena, and sad to say, even some Christian schools would get a low grade when it comes to teaching character principles and moral values.

That was not the case 200 years ago with our Founding Fathers. In fact, Noah Webster (1758–1843), America's most influential educator in the age that our nation was founded, stated:

> Education, in great measure, forms the moral characters of men, and morals are the basis of government. Education should therefore be the first care of a legislature; not merely the institution of schools, but the furnishing of them with the best men for teachers. A good system of education should be the first article in the code of political regulations; for it is much easier to introduce and establish an effectual system for preserving morals, than to correct by penal statutes the ill effects of a bad system. The goodness of a heart is of infinitely more consequence to society than an elegance of manners; nor will any superficial accomplishments repair the want of principle in the mind. It is always better to be vulgarly right than politely wrong.[1]

In one of his famous "Blue-backed Spellers" Webster included a *Moral Catechism*—rules upon which to base moral conduct."[2]

This is the kind of Christian education America needs to get back to, and with this book my good friend Dick Mayhue has provided the Christian community with an excellent tool for gleaning and teaching godly character and moral principles from the lives of men and women in the Bible, which is why God gave them to us—for our admonition and learning (1 Corinthians 10:11).

More than that, the book is interesting and contains a great deal of practical application for Christians of this age and culture. I am confident that parents, pastors, teachers, and all Christians will find this book to be a good investment. I heartily recommend it both for your reading enjoyment and for teaching purposes.

Tim LaHaye

INTRODUCTION

MY SPECIAL FRIEND John MacArthur uniquely described to a group of pastors his progressive realization that the ministry was tough. "At first," he said, "the ministry was just plain fun. So much so I could not understand why so many men struggled." Continuing on, John described how it later became hard work to prepare two new messages a week and oversee a growing church. "Finally I discovered the ministry was an intense spiritual battle with Satan over the souls of people."

Life is no different. The dailies of living involve warfare against a number of enemies like Satan, life circumstances, other people, and even ourselves. My experience in Vietnam continually reminds me that, realistically, life is just like the war zone. Everyone is shooting at me and I am fighting like mad to stay alive.

Years ago I taught a group of young boys about the great heroes of God in the Bible. I concluded by asking, "Wouldn't you like to be a spiritual giant for God too?" Everyone shouted, "Yes!" except the boy standing next to me who replied, "Naw, I don't want to have anything to do with that stuff."

They hadn't prepared me in seminary for that kind of response. So I answered with the most intelligent words I could think of, "Why not?" The boy instantly shot back, "Because the bigger they are, the harder they fall."

He had a good point. Life is a battle and the casualty rate is high. Just as I was about to panic over how to recover the lesson, a Scripture came to mind. "The steps of a man are established by the Lord; and He delights in his way. When he falls, he shall not be hurled headlong; because the Lord is the One who holds his hand" (Ps. 37:23-24).

My young friend, the skeptic, became a believer when he realized that God would be on his side. If he fell, God would be there to help him recover. I've never forgotten that episode because it so poignantly describes the Christian life.

Listen to Jahaziel who delivered a striking message to King Jehoshaphat. "Do not fear or be dismayed . . . for the battle is not yours but God's" (2 Chron. 20:15). By viewing the Christian life from this eternal perspective and by fighting on earth according to God's battle plan, anyone can be on the winning side and successfully fight life's daily battles to spiritual victory.

In living out our Christianity, there is no better place to go than the Bible for help in developing a strategy to be on God's winning side. Romans 15:4 strikes this chord. "For whatever was written in earlier times was written for our instruction, that through perseverance and the encouragement of the Scriptures we might have hope." (15:4)

A Christian's Survival Guide looks back to earlier times to men and women who fought the battle of life. Some lost, some were wounded, while others tasted victory without knowing the agony of defeat or the pain of being wounded. Some were winners; some losers. But they all fought battles—there were no exceptions. Their enemies remain our opponents today. These Old Testament warriors teach us contemporary lessons that are loaded with twentieth-century reality.

Some combatants like Judas or Ananias and Sapphira looked like certain winners but lost. Others, like Matthew and Paul, occupied "the loser's circle" for the first part of their lives but later finished as notable victors.

Solomon, Jonah, Eve, and Saul faced the same enemies that we do today. They possessed all of the resources to conquer their foes. Sadly, the Bible reports that they lost. These people, who walked on feet of clay as we do, serve to warn us that victory is not certain unless we stay close by God's side and obey God's Word.

Others fell while fighting but later recovered to win. Their ranks include Elijah, Samson, Habakkuk, and Moses. They stumbled and fell, but in the midst of an awkward tumble, they reached out for God and He caught them before they crashed. Each life shouts, "There is hope!" to you who are down but not yet out.

By God's grace some fought and never fell. This enviable crew numbers Joseph, Job, Ruth, and Daniel among their kind. It's possible to win without being wounded. These heroes of the faith encourage us to enter the battle and to keep fighting for God's glory.

I once read that the only way to lose is to quit. If I could write the epitaph of our lives, it would read, "They won by failing . . . to quit."

David Hubbard exactingly captures the spirit of *A Christian's Survival Guide*.

> The program of God through history is like a relay race. Let one runner drop out and the whole team loses. Let one runner lose the baton and the whole team is eliminated. Let one runner break the rules and the whole team is disqualified. The work of no runner counts until every runner does his share and the anchor man has hit the tape at the finish line.
>
> The phrase 'let us keep our eyes fixed on Jesus' is the key. The idea is clear. There are lots of distractions as we run. Bypaths beckon us; false goals attract us; competition discourages us; opposition causes us to falter. Jesus, however, a tried and trusted leader who blazed the trail of faith by His own obedience and perseverance and who finished the course in a burst of glory is both our guide and our goal. We look away from everything else to Him, if we want to run well.[1]

Let's pray together that we will run well for God's glory and thus be on the winning side.

PART ONE

Warning: Some Failed to Win

ONE

SOLOMON:
The Shipwrecked Saint

SOLOMON'S KINGDOM WAS the *Titanic* among Hebrew reigns. He was wealthy and wise; his kingdom enjoyed unprecedented peace, promise, and prosperity. Israel seemed unsinkable.

God had warned the captain about life's navigational hazards, but with wild abandon, Solomon ordered "full speed ahead." Violent collisions with four devastating "icebergs" resulted. The good ship Israel capsized and the hopes of God's blessing sank with her.

These are the lessons to look for as we are warned by the unexpected commentary on Solomon's life in the Book of Ecclesiastes.

HIS ENEMY: SELF-INDULGENCE
HIS WARNINGS: MISAPPROPRIATION OF WISDOM, WEALTH, AND WOMEN FOR PERSONAL GAIN RATHER THAN FOR GOD'S GLORY
HIS FATAL BLOW: WHEN GOD WAS NO LONGER THE UNIQUE OBJECT OF PERSONAL WORSHIP

At 2:20 A.M. on April 15, 1912, the impossible happened. The unsinkable ship sank. The most celebrated cruise ship in all of history nose-dived to the Atlantic bottom. It had sailed four days earlier from North Hampton, England on its maiden voyage en route to New York; no expense had been spared to make it the most gala cruise ever. All went according to schedule until Sunday night when the *Titanic* sailed into an ice field.

She had received four warnings of impending danger that day from ships who were in the midst of the ice, but she chose to ignore all four—several did not even reach the bridge or the captain. At 11:00 P.M. that Sunday night the wireless operator, John Phillips, received a direct warning call from the *California* which was ten miles away in the midst of some very large ice.

Phillips was tired, having sent messages all day to America. So that night he cavalierly tapped back, "Shut up, shut up, I'm busy." Forty minutes later the beloved ship of the White Star Line collided with an ice behemoth.

Within hours she rested in her watery grave along with 1,500 passengers and crew, certainly one of the world's great human disasters. The sinking of Israel with Solomon at the helm ranks as one of the world's great spiritual disasters.

In the Book of Ecclesiastes Solomon recounts the horrors of collision at sea as a caution to you and me who sail the same waters. In order for us to grasp what Solomon is saying, I want to summarize the contents of Ecclesiastes to give us a framework for our thinking.

Ecclesiastes is a despairing autobiography written by Solomon in his twilight years. Here he rehearses the utter uselessness of squandering God's means and wealth to accomplish personal ends and to add to earthly pleasures. He begins with this well-known phrase, "Vanity of vanities! All is vanity" (Ecc. 1:2). That's the way he ends, "Vanity of vanities...all is vanity" (12:8). What a tragedy in the life of Solomon!

The question we want to answer is, How did the glorious and seemingly invincible King Solomon and his kingdom Israel come to such a disastrous end? By application, we need to ask ourselves, What can we learn from Solomon so that our lives never reproduce the pitiful portrait we see painted in the Book of Ecclesiastes? Pay careful attention as Solomon sounds the alarm against these four icebergs: misdirected wisdom, misused wealth, multiplied women, and mixed worship.

God gave David concerning his son one of the greatest promises in the Bible. "When your days are complete and you lie down with your fathers . . . I will establish his kingdom. He shall build a house for My name, and I will establish the throne of his kingdom forever" (2 Sam. 7:12-13).

On his deathbed, David gallantly passed that charge on to his son Solomon:

> As David's time to die drew near, he charged Solomon his son, saying, "I am going the way of all the earth. Be strong, therefore, and show yourself a man. And keep the charge of the Lord your God, to walk in His ways, to keep His statutes, His commandments, His ordinances, and His testimonies, according to what is written in the law of Moses, that you may succeed in all that you do and wherever you turn, so that the Lord may carry out His promise which He spoke concerning me, saying, 'If your sons are careful of their way, to walk before Me in truth with all their heart and with all their soul, you shall not lack a man on the throne of Israel.' " (1 Kings 2:1-4)

God then personally delivered that message to Solomon in a dream (1 Kings 3:14). If all of that wasn't enough, we read in 1 Kings 8 about Solomon dedicating the temple for the entire nation, where he prays the very same promises that God had given to him. Then God reappeared to Solomon to restate and reaffirm these promises to Solomon.

Not only did Solomon hold the *promises* that God had given to him, but he also held the *precepts* that had been given to the prophets before Solomon, in particular those of Moses who wrote the first five books in our Old Testament. There God gave Moses a record for future kings—the very precepts that should have guarded Solomon from coming near any one of the succession of four icebergs with which he collided.

God had clearly said, "Don't misdirect My wisdom." The way to have a wise reign for Israel was not only to know the Word of God, but day by day to be in it, reading it and knowing it (Deut. 17:18-20). Kings were also not to aggressively seek wealth, and the king was to set the example for the entire kingdom and walk in the ways that God had ordained for Adam and Eve, having a monogamous marriage. "Moreover, he shall not multiply horses for himself, nor shall he cause the people to return to Egypt to multiply horses, since the Lord has said to you, 'You shall never again return that way.' Neither shall he multiply wives for himself, lest his heart turn away; nor shall he greatly increase silver and gold for himself " (Deut. 17:16-17). The Scriptures also were clear that the nation and the king, setting the example, were to be uncompromisingly devoted to Almighty God (Deut. 17:2-5).

So God said, "If you want a pure kingdom, there are four things to avoid. Misdirected wisdom, misused wealth, multiplied women, and finally, mixed worship." Solomon had *promises;* Solomon had *precepts*. He also published these among his 3,000 *proverbs* in the book that we call Proverbs. He ably warned others about the very icebergs that eventually caused his ruin.

How did it happen? How could Solomon have blown it and missed all that God gave him? How did Solomon ever end up as a shipwrecked saint? Be warned of this—it did happen to Solomon and it can happen to us.

Turn to Ecclesiastes 1 where Solomon recounts the horrors of his tragically sinful life. We want to chart a course that will cause us to miss the dangerous icebergs that sank the ship of Israel with Solomon at her helm.

MISDIRECTED WISDOM

Solomon says the first iceberg to be circumvented is misdirected wisdom. One day God appeared to Solomon in a dream (1 Kings 3:3-14) and asked, in effect, "If you could have anything you wanted, ask for it, because I'm so minded to give it to you" (v. 5).

Solomon responded, "I'd like to have wisdom to judge between good and evil and to rule the nation of Israel in Your stead, Lord" (v. 9).

SOLOMON: THE SHIPWRECKED SAINT

God said, "You've answered so well and so faithfully that not only will I give you the wisdom, but I'll give you wealth and peace and prosperity and all the rest that goes with the kingdom."
Wisdom was bestowed upon Solomon (vv. 10-13). He was able to discern the difference between good and evil, to lead the nation, and to become the wisest man who had ever lived in that time or who ever would live in all time. He gained an international reputation (4:29-34); people came from all around to look in wonder at the wisdom of Solomon and to see if, in fact, it was actually true.

He truly matched up to the claims that went out from the kingdom. He was everything that God had intended him to be, and seemingly, a little bit more. What happened?
Let's read Ecclesiastes 1:13-18.

And I set my mind to seek and explore by wisdom concerning all that has been done under heaven. It is a grievous task which God has given to the sons of men to be afflicted with. I have seen all the works which have been done under the sun, and behold, all is vanity and striving after wind. What is crooked cannot be straightened, and what is lacking cannot be counted. I said to myself, "Behold, I have magnified and increased wisdom more than all who were over Jerusalem before me; and my mind has observed a wealth of wisdom and knowledge." And I set my mind to know wisdom and to know madness and folly; I realized that this also is striving after wind. Because in much wisdom there is much grief, and increasing knowledge results in increasing pain.

Remember that Solomon was looking back at life from his later years and telling us what it had been like. All of the wisdom that God had given him brought only emptiness. It didn't satisfy. It was vanity.
Why such a strange response? I believe that Solomon was unsatisfied to minister the wisdom that God had given him by revelation; rather, he tested God's wisdom by human reason and empirical research. Solomon misdirected the wisdom and went beyond God's intention. He emasculated the wisdom of God. He

stretched it all out of proportion. When that was done, he had seemingly dethroned God and deified man. God had never intended for any of that to happen.

One commentator paraphrased the words of Solomon, "I did succeed in becoming a great man, so had access to resources that others did not have. And besides, I grew in wisdom above all that had ever been before me over the people of God, in fact, by honest mental effort I added to the natural capacities that God had given me, acquiring 'wisdom and knowledge' in abundance."[1]

Solomon, like so many human intellectuals, struggled for an entire lifetime to scale the mountains of learning. Then in the last days of his life, exhausted by the journey, he pulled himself over the last obstacles only to meet face to face with Almighty God, who had been sitting there for all eternity. Solomon let loose an unforgettable cry.

> Then I said to myself, "As is the fate of the fool, it will also befall me. Why then have I been extremely wise?" So I said to myself, "This too is vanity." For there is no lasting remembrance of the wise man as with the fool, inasmuch as in the coming days all will be forgotten. And how the wise man and the fool alike die! So I hated life, for the work which had been done under the sun was grievous to me; because everything is futility and striving after wind." (Ecc. 2:15-17)

What a sad commentary on a person's life. As he looked back he had the promises; he had the precepts which he affirmed as true in Proverbs, but he failed to practice them and thus misdirected the wisdom God gave him. So he wrote, "People learn from me. It's empty; it's useless; it brings tears to my eyes and pain to my heart. Be warned. Don't walk where I walked. Don't live as I lived. Accept God's wisdom by faith; don't test it. Use it with an eternal perspective to know good rather than with an earthly view to know the pain and folly of evil."

MISUSED WEALTH

From misdirected wisdom the other three icebergs broke off. The second iceberg is misused wealth. Someone remarked recently that the futility of riches is stated very plainly in two places—in our income tax forms and in our Bibles. But no one says it better than King Solomon in Ecclesiastes 2:1-11.

First Kings gives us a few insights into the riches and wealth of Solomon's life. First Kings 4:25 tells us that Solomon had amassed 40,000 horses. Peace reigned on all borders of his kingdom, which started in the east from the Euphrates, continued to the west on the Mediterranean and extended all the way south to Egypt (5:4). In 1 Kings 7:1-8, we learn about the bungalow he built for himself and his wife. The completion took 13 years—twice as long as it took him to build the house of God. He was the richest and wisest man on the globe. People came from the four corners of the earth and added to his wealth by bringing gifts to him (10:23-25).

First Kings 10:27 contains this interesting sentence: "The king made silver as common as stones in Jerusalem." The parallel passage in 2 Chronicles 1:15 notes that both silver and gold were so multiplied and so plenteous that they were just as common as the little pebbles in the stream. Not only that, but he made cedars as plentiful as sycamore trees. The Lebanon cedars talked about here were the parallel to the sequoia redwoods in California. Imagine sequoia redwoods in everybody's backyard. And it all belonged to Solomon.

What a tremendous kingdom. He had houses, vineyards, parks, fruit trees, ponds, slaves, herds, treasures, singers, and concubines. You name it, he had it. We can't begin to imagine what Solomon's life was like and what God had given to him. I've come to the conclusion that the most sorry life in all of the Bible, second only to Judas, is the life of Solomon. He had all of the delights, all of the provisions, and all of the revelation of God, yet he perverted these to use them on himself rather than for God.

The real key to understanding Solomon's heart is found in Ecclesiastes 2:1-11. I want to point out a couple of phrases in the text that expose Solomon's heart in his earlier years. Solomon said to himself, "I will test you with pleasure," instead of allowing God to test him (2:1). In verse 3 he said, in effect, "I'm going to explore for all the things that are done under heaven." You know where his mind should have been? Not on the things of earth but on the things above—on the things of God.

Listen to Solomon's boasts, "I made ... parks for myself" (2:5). "I made ponds of water for myself" (2:6). He tested and experienced the pleasures of men (2:8). Then he talks about not withholding from his heart anything sensuous, undisciplined, or reckless (2:10). Following that he cries out and tells us what it accomplished. "Thus I considered all my activities which my hands had done and the labor which I had exerted, and behold all was vanity and striving after wind and there was no profit under the sun" (2:11).

Solomon had misused his God-given wealth to satisfy himself rather than asking the question, How can I invest in God's kingdom for God's glory and for the good of God's people?

There is nothing wrong with wealth. However, when we think we obtained it ourselves, it becomes bad. We begin to spend it on ourselves with utter disregard for the plans of the One who gave it to us. That was the downfall of Solomon. He became self-satisfied and self-consumed.

MULTIPLIED WOMEN

Now we come to the third iceberg, which was the beginning of the end for Solomon, for his sons, and for the kingdom of Israel. He recklessly crashed into the iceberg of multiplied women.

> And I discovered more bitter than death the woman whose heart is snares and nets, whose hands are chains. One who is pleasing to God will escape from her, but the sinner will be captured by her. "Behold, I have discovered this," says the Preacher, "adding one thing to another to find an explanation, which I am still seeking but have not found. I have found one man among a thousand, but I have not found a woman among all these. Behold, I have found only this, that God made men upright, but they have sought out many devices." (Ecc. 7:26-29)

Where did Solomon come up with these words of woe? He followed a long line of men previous to him, who had multiplied women. You can read about Lamech, Abraham, Esau, Jacob, Moses, Gideon, Elkanah, Saul, and Solomon's father, David.

Before he became king, Solomon married a woman whose name was Naamah (2 Chron. 12:13). She was an Ammonite princess who became the mother of Rehoboam, who later became king of the Southern Kingdom when God violently ripped the kingdom in two. After Solomon had been crowned king of Israel, he formed a political alliance with Pharaoh of Egypt, who ruled to the south. As part of the culture of that day, he married one of Pharaoh's daughters to seal the covenant treaty (1 Kings 3:1). When all of the efforts of Solomon to secure peace and to satisfy his sensual lust had come to an end, he had accumulated no less than 700 wives and 300 concubines (1 Kings 11:3).

This is background to Ecclesiastes 7. Few, if any, of the 1,000 women whom he had associated himself with had proven to be righteous. He married outside of the nation, and he married for reasons other than those God had given. From the time he married the second wife, he lived in utter disregard for that which God had given in the Book of Genesis. "For this cause a man shall leave his father and his mother, and shall cleave to his wife; and they shall become one flesh (Gen. 2:24).

In disobedience to God's Word, he had married all of these foreign women who were outside of the faith (Ex. 34:12-16; Deut. 7:1-3; Josh. 23:12-13). Here's a great lesson for those who entertain ideas of evangelistic dating. "I'll just date this good-looking guy (or gal) who doesn't know Christ and sooner or later they'll come to the Saviour." Let Solomon be a stern warning: don't date outside the faith, much less marry outside the faith.

The most indicting statement of Solomon's marital affairs came from the pen of Nehemiah 500 years after Solomon's reign. "Did not Solomon King of Israel sin regarding these things? Yet among the many nations there was no king like him, and he was loved by his God, and God made him king over all Israel; nevertheless the foreign women caused even him to sin" (Neh. 13:26).

Not long ago I was reading about William Jennings Bryan and his dating years. He met a lovely young lady, fell in love with her, and decided the right thing to do was to go and ask her father for her hand in marriage. He knew that her dad had strong religious beliefs, so he thought it might be nice to quote some Scripture. He quoted from Solomon in Proverbs 18:22: "He who finds a wife finds a good thing." The father responded from Paul, "He that marrieth doeth well. But he that marrieth not, doeth better." The young man went back to Solomon who had 700 wives. Therefore, Paul ought to be the better expert about getting married.

If William Jennings Bryan were alive today, I would direct him to Ecclesiastes 9:9 where Solomon, sobered by his waning years, reaffirms the sanctity of a one-woman relationship in marriage. "Enjoy life with the woman whom you love all the days of your fleeting life which He has given to you under the sun; for this is your reward in life, and in your toil in which you have labored under the sun." Solomon said, "Guys, the greatest reward you're going to get out of life is the wife that God gives you."

MIXED WORSHIP

There's one more iceberg we need to examine. Solomon, through his multiplied wives, made himself fatally vulnerable to the crashing waves of God's coming wrath as he hit the berg of mixed worship. Everybody knows the name of Solomon, which means peace or peaceful, but few know him as God knew him. God gave Solomon a special name (2 Sam. 12:25); it was *Jedediah*, which means "beloved of the Lord." That is very endearing—almost as intimate as "this is My beloved Son," which God said of the Lord Jesus Christ. And yet, it was this very one, beloved of the Lord, who prostituted his covenant relationship with God. Following the lead of his wives, he went after strange gods. Solomon wrote about it in Ecclesiastes 5:1-7.

Let me fill in some background for you. First Kings 11:4-8 tells us that in his later years his multiplied wives turned his heart away from Almighty God and directed it to worship dead idols. He built temples in Jerusalem to worship the Astoreth, Milcom, Chemosh, and Molech. He built a house of worship for most known idols of the day. Jerusalem turned from a place that was devoted to the worship of Jehovah God to one that was so polluted that Jehovah was almost unrecognizable in the worship life of the kingdom. Solomon violated the first three of God's Ten Commandments. He had other gods (Ex. 20:3). He made graven images (Ex. 20:4). To top that, Solomon made vows and took the name of the Lord in vain (Ex. 20:7).

God's patience came to an end; His mercy ceased.

> So the Lord said to Solomon, "Because you have done this, and you have not kept My covenant and My statutes, which I have commanded you, I will surely tear the kingdom from you, and will give it to your servant. Nevertheless I will not do it in your days for the sake of your father David, but I will tear it out of the hand of your son. However, I will not tear away all the kingdom, but I will give one tribe to your son for the sake of My servant David and for the sake of Jerusalem which I have chosen" (1 Kings 11:11-13).

What a sad day for Solomon! This man's wisdom was so great that Jesus compared Himself to Solomon in Matthew 12:42 when He said, "Something greater than Solomon is here." Solomon's wealth had so exceeded that of others that Solomon was the only fair comparison in Matthew 6:29 when Jesus extolled the riches of God's created world. This great man lost his kingdom.

That is why Solomon says in Ecclesiastes 5, "Learn from my mistakes; I will tell you the vanity of the sacrifice of the fools. Make sure your worship is right and pure. Let me tell you the emptiness of multiplied words and dreams. Walk into the presence of God and know that He, and He alone, is holy."

Take special note of his words in Ecclesiastes 5:7. "For in many dreams and in many words there is emptiness." The last three words are so important: "Rather, fear God." That was the instruction given in Deuteronomy 17:19, to fear God by obeying His commandments.

It's the thread that's woven through the Book of Ecclesiastes, "I know that everything God does will remain forever; there is nothing to add to it and there is nothing to take from it, for God has so worked that men should fear Him" (3:14). "It is good that you grasp one thing, and also not let go of the other; for the one who fears God comes forth with both of them" (7:18). "Although a sinner does evil a hundred times and may lengthen his life, still I know that it will be well for those who fear God, who fear Him openly" (8:12).

Solomon brought the book to a close at 12:13-14. In his last years, he recognized how wrong he had been. He repented of his sin and once again was right with God. Solomon warned about the miserable failures of his life, and that warning has been preserved for almost 3,000 years. "The conclusion, when all has been heard, is: fear God and keep His commandments, because this applies to every person. Because God will bring every act to judgment, everything which is hidden, whether it is good or evil."

AN IMPORTANT THOUGHT

One final question: how is it with you in the areas of wisdom, wealth, women, and worship? Let me summarize what God expects of us. Here is what God will one day judge good, if it's the pattern or habit of our life: a faith response to God's revelation that needs no human reason or empirical research for verification; a pilgrim's perspective on wealth, which recognizes that it comes from God; we spend it for God's glory by investing it in the works of the Lord instead of the passing pleasures of life; a one-woman mentality, which preserves the purity of marriage and the dignity of women; an uncompromising devotion to God and God alone— nothing added to dilute, nothing taken away to diminish. These four qualities are the proof of fearing God. If these are part and parcel of our lives, they will be judged as good when our deeds are judged.

I close with an instructive story about the life of a man whom God used greatly. He too faced the ice fields that confronted Solomon. Charles Finney, a well-known evangelist in America, began as a young lawyer in the state of New York. As he sat early one morning in the law office, God's quiet voice began to ask him, "Finney, what are you going to do when you finish your course?" He thought a minute and responded, "Well, I think I'll put out a shingle and practice law." God responded, "Then what?" Finney said, "I'll get rich." "Then what?" "Oh, I think I'll retire," "Then what?" "I'll probably die." "Then what?" "Judgment."

As the word *judgment* was uttered from the lips of Finney, he was brought to a recognition that all that he did in life would one day be brought before the bar of God, and judgment would be rendered either for or against. He was so moved by that experience that he immediately dedicated his life and his entire being to Jesus Christ.

If we follow Finney's lead, we'll miss the icebergs that sank Israel. We'll never be scratched and scarred as was the shipwrecked saint because we've chosen to fear God and obey His commandments. "The fear of the Lord is the beginning of wisdom, and the knowledge of the Holy One is understanding" (Prov. 9:10).

TWO

JONAH:
The Wrong-Way Prophet

MYSTERY SURROUNDS JONAH. Although we know nothing of them, his early tests of faith must have been passed with flying colors. Thus God trusted Jonah with a challenging spiritual assignment to be His ambassador among the Assyrians.

Totally out of character, Jonah zooms off the wrong way on a one-way street to Nineveh. By the time God pulls him over and reverses his course, Jonah's heart is permanently set in a cement called cold indifference.

A number of obvious symptoms mark Jonah. Use them to give yourself a "spiritual" at home. Through this means of early detection, you can avoid a terminal case of "Jonah's disease."

This summary sets the stage for us to learn from Jonah's mistakes.

HIS ENEMY: CARNALITY
HIS WARNINGS: INDIFFERENCE AND DISOBEDIENCE TOWARD GOD AND GOD'S WILL
HIS FATAL BLOW: CONSTANT ANGER AT GOD

The life of Jonah is like a picture with nine things wrong in it. We want to identify these flaws so that they never become a part of our own Christian experience. Jonah was like the believers in Corinth who walked as mere men (1 Cor. 3:3). If either Jonah or the Corinthians had been arrested because of their faith in God, there would not have been enough evidence to successfully convict them of the charges.

Jonah is not a mythical person (Jonah 1:1). He lived and served God as a prophet in the eighth century B.C. "He restored the border of Israel from the entrance of Hamath as far as the Sea of the Arabah, according to the word of the Lord, the God of Israel, which He spoke through His servant Jonah the son of Amittai, the prophet, who was of Gath-hepher." (2 Kings 14:25). Jesus authenticates the historical reality of Jonah by comparing His time in the grave with Jonah's time in the large fish (Matt. 12:40).

Jonah joined Amos in the prophetic ranks; both were involved with messages to Assyria, the ruling world empire of their day. Amos told how Assyria, as God's instrument of wrath for unchecked sin, would ravage Israel. In contrast, Jonah bore a message of repentance to Nineveh. His job was to evangelize the city.

Nineveh, situated on the eastern bank of the Tigris River, served as the ancient capital of the Assyrian Empire. It was reportedly the largest city in the then-known world. It's variously estimated that Nineveh's population ranged from 600,000 to 1 million people.

The Lord commands Jonah to penetrate this significant city with God's cry against their wickedness (1:1-2). He is to go to Israel's archenemy and present the message of repentance based on God's grace, compassion, and loving-kindness. What transpires from Jonah 1:3 to 4:11 is shocking and unexpected. Yet in our own humanness, we have all had Jonah-like experiences. Thus we come not to condemn him but to learn and be warned.

RUNNING FROM GOD

Jonah should have been running with God; instead he ran away from Him. Jonah altered his travel schedule from Nineveh to

Tarshish. He should have gone east but ended up heading west. Greek historian Herodotus identified Tarshish as a port in Spain. Our prophet is attempting the impossible because God is everywhere (Ps. 139:7-10; Amos 9:2-3). Why did Jonah run? There are probably at least two reasons. First, Jonah knew that Assyria would later destroy Israel. He knew that from reading Hosea 5:13; 7:11; 8:8-9; 10:6; and 11:5. Isaiah preached the same message (Isa. 8:6-8). Undoubtedly Jonah's fierce national pride clouded his commitment to God's divine appointment.

Also, Jonah knew well the despicable character and conduct of the Assyrians. They acted with barbarian vengeance.

> No considerations of pity were permitted to stand in the way of Assyrian policy. It could not afford to garrison its conquests, and it practised a plan which largely dispensed with the necessity for leaving garrisons behind the Assyrian armies. There was unsparing slaughter to begin with. The kings seem to gloat in their inscriptions over the spectacle presented by the field of battle. They describe how it was covered with the corpses of the vanquished. This carnage was followed up by fiendish inflictions upon individual cities. The leading men, as at Lachish when Sennacherib had conquered that city, were led forth, seized by the executioners, and subjected to various punishments, all of them filled to the brim with horror.[1]

Jonah must have thought that their deeds were overwhelmingly evil and thus that they were unable to receive God's forgiveness—even if they repented.

These same thoughts can cloud this issue for us. We, like Jonah, have been given a commission—the Great Commission. It's mentioned once in each of the first five books of the New Testament (Matt. 28:18-20; Mark 16:15; Luke 24:46-47; John 20:21; Acts 1:8). We are commanded to "go ... and make disciples of all the nations" (Matt. 28:19).

As you look at the picture of Jonah's life, look also at yourself. Are you running with God or away from Him? Do you see yourself as Paul saw himself—the foremost of sinners (1 Tim. 1:15) and the least of saints? (Eph. 3:8) With that perspective, everyone else is more worthy of the Gospel than we are.

SILENT ABOUT GOD

There must have been something special about Jonah. Instead of dispatching another prophet, God tracks Jonah down with a raging storm to reverse his course (1:4). The storm was so violent that the veteran sailors knew survival went beyond their own seafaring skills. They cried out to the pagan gods of the day and retreated to the last human resort of jettisoning cargo.

By this time Jonah should have been praying to the source of the storm—the living God. Astute prophet that he was, Jonah should have put two and two together. It would seem obvious that Jonah's disobedience had resulted in God's attention getter.

Jonah looked more like an atheist than anyone on the ship. Yet he likely was the only believer. While the sailors prayed and struggled, Jonah slept. The captain finally had to come and ask Jonah to pray also. The pagans cast lots to see who had sinned. Although they did not know God, God intervened and pointed the finger at Jonah. "The lot is cast into the lap, but its every decision is from the Lord" (Prov. 16:33).

With Jonah identified as the culprit, the crew bombarded him with questions. Cornered by the storm and the angry sailors, Jonah finally acknowledged his God as the Creator God—the One who made the sea and controlled their condition. Only under the most arduous conditions did Jonah finally admit he related to the living God.

He was a "secret service" Christian. You couldn't even yank it out of him. He was much like the converted priests of Jesus' day (John 12:42-43) and even Joseph of Arimathea (John 19:38). What does it take for you to tell others that Jesus is Lord? Are you openly testifying of Christ's grace in your life? Our mandate is to be ready and willing to speak of our hope (1 Peter 3:15-16).

Finally Jonah spilled the beans, and the sailors sought his counsel on how to end the storm. At first they rejected Jonah's solution. After trying once more to ensure their own safety, they prayed and took Jonah's original advice and threw him overboard.

While Jonah should have acted as their priest to make intercession for them, they acted as their own priests. Jonah became the sacrifice and was fed to the sea (1:16-17).

PRAYING ONLY UNDER DURESS

Prayer is always in. We are to pray without ceasing (1 Thes. 5:17). But there is something radically wrong with Jonah. Instead of praying for courage to obey God's will, the Assyrians' repentance, or the safety of the sailors, Jonah does not start praying until he finds himself in an impossible situation.

Jonah became a "whale belly" prayer warrior. When I was in Vietnam, we called people like Jonah foxhole Christians. They were concerned with God only when their own lives were in danger.

Jonah's is a wonderful prayer. It seems to evidence a repentant heart (2:4). Jonah seems to renew his commitment (2:7-9). The joy of Jonah's salvation seemingly has returned (2:9). So God answers Jonah's prayer and causes the fish to vomit Jonah up on shore (2:10).

This is where many can't buy all of the Jonah story. They can't believe in the sovereignty of God to appoint a fish (1:17), to preserve Jonah alive, and to rescue him for further ministry (2:10). However, let me assure you that every word here is true.

Over the years several accounts of men being swallowed by great fish have come to light. If your faith wavers here, let me give you a little historical light so you can walk for a moment by sight. In one incident in February 1891, a sailor named James Bartley was swallowed by a large sperm whale, unbeknownst to his fellow whaling ship crew members. The next morning, the whale's stomach was hoisted onto the ship's deck.

> According to M. de Parville, science editor of the *Journal des Debats*, who investigated the incident, there was then a movement in the whale's belly. When it was opened, Bartley was found unconscious. He was carried on deck and bathed in sea water. This revived him, but his mind was not clear and he was confined to the captain's quarters for two weeks, behaving like a lunatic.

Within four weeks, Bartley had fully recovered and related what it had been like to live in the belly of a whale. He remembered the whale's tail hitting his boat. Then, reported de Parville, Bartley was encompassed in darkness and felt himself slipping along a smooth passage. His hands felt something slimy all around him. The heat was unbearable—it was thought to be 104 degrees—and he lost consciousness. When he awoke, he was in the captain's cabin.

For the rest of his life, Bartley's face, neck and hands remained white, bleached by the whale's gastric juices.[2]

So far Jonah has been unmistakenly consistent in his walk with God: he ran from God; he was silent about God; and he prayed only under duress. These are key signs that for some reason Jonah's attention focused more on himself and less on God. He had forsaken the testimony of the psalmist who wrote, "I have set the Lord continually before me; because He is at my right hand, I will not be shaken" (Ps. 16:8).

Stop a moment and ask yourself, "Where is my focus?" Is it on heaven or earth? Is it on God or self? Does it value the temporary or the eternal?

PREACHING UNDER PROTEST

God's grace proved greater for Jonah. What he did not want God to grant to the Assyrians, God granted to Jonah. Jonah received a reprieve—he had a second chance to redeem his prophetic ministry.

Jonah had no other choice. His worst fears were realized—revival broke out in Nineveh (3:5). God, true to His word, relented when the Assyrians repented.

Jonah played the role of God's human instrument to bring about one of the world's great revivals. The impact of Jonah's preaching in Nineveh at least equaled Peter's preaching at Pentecost (Acts 2:14-42).

All seemed well on the outside, but Jonah was still not right on the inside. His head was in it, but his heart had never joined the matter. He had yet to understand that God is more concerned with attitudes than He is with actions. "For I delight in loyalty rather than sacrifice, and in the knowledge of God rather than burnt offering" (Hosea 6:6).

ANGRY WITH GOD

If any doubts remain that Jonah's relationship with God had grown stale, Jonah's displeasure with the Assyrians' response to his preaching and his anger at God proves the point. God is the One who should have been angry. Jonah should have known that "it is a terrifying thing to fall into the hands of the living God" (Heb. 10:31).

Jonah needed Paul's advice when he wrote, "Rejoice in the Lord always; again I will say, rejoice!" (Phil. 4:4) He needed to camp at Psalm 16:11: "Thou wilt make known to me the path of life; in Thy presence is fulness of joy; in Thy right hand there are pleasures forever."

CONFUSED ABOUT LIFE

Jonah joins the ranks of Job (Job 6:8-9), Moses (Num. 11:10-15), and Elijah (1 Kings 19:4), all of whom asked God to take their lives. This is only Jonah's second prayer in the book. The first time he prayed for God to save him (2:1-9). Now he prays for God to kill him (4:3, 8).

From Jonah's perspective, life is no longer worth living. He can't adjust to God's perspective, so he holds an "abandon ship drill" on living. Even a minor catastrophe like his shade tree's dying caused him to go off the deep end.

Let's stop here for a minute. Could it possibly be you are in the pits like Jonah? The hole is so deep you have to look up to see the bottom? Maybe you are even contemplating suicide. Perhaps you are praying to God, "Death is better to me than life." If your life matches up with Jonah's, you need some help. Let me suggest you confide in your spouse or a faithful friend. It could be the occasion for a visit to your family physician or a Christian counselor. If you are despairing, don't hike on in life alone. Look to someone now as a source of comfort and strength.

WATCHING INSTEAD OF WORKING

A young reporter once asked the great Oklahoma University football coach, Bud Wilkinson, "What makes football the great game that it is?" The coach thought for a minute and then fired back a shocking answer. "Football isn't all that great, because it's a sport with 100,000 people in the stands desperately needing exercise while there are 22 men on the field desperately needing rest."

Wilkinson pointed out that football was a spectator sport. That's what Jonah's walk with God had been. He went to the east side of Nineveh to spectate. Instead, he should have continued to participate.

People on the sidelines tend to throw rocks when a play does not go their way. Those in the game don't have time because they are too busy figuring out the next play. Christianity is not a spectator sport. God never intended us to "soak, sour, and spoil." Rather, He wrote through Peter, "As each one has received a special gift, employ it in serving one another, as good stewards of the manifold grace of God" (1 Peter 4:10).

If you are not in the game, you need to be—somewhere. See your pastor so that you don't end up living as a bitter bench sitter rather than an excited contributor to building Christ's church.

ARGUING WITH GOD

In response to Jonah's anger, God asks twice, "Do you have a good reason to be angry?" (4:4, 9) The first time it was over the eternal souls of men, the second over a plant that had provided Jonah a brief moment of relief.

The obvious answer to God's question is no. But Jonah answers, "Yes, I have." Jonah's will is at odds with God's will. He doesn't possess the spirit of Christ, who affirmed, "Yet not as I will, but as Thou wilt" (Matt. 26:39).

Job learned his lesson when he tried to take on God. Listen to this strong rebuke from the Lord. "Who is this that darkens counsel by words without knowledge? Now gird up your loins like a man, and I will ask you, and you instruct Me!" (Job 38:2-3) It is as silly as the clay telling the potter how to make a pot (Rom. 9:20-21). So it is ludicrous for the creation to instruct the Creator. If you can identify with Jonah here, then listen carefully to what Paul wrote to the Roman church.

> What if God, although willing to demonstrate His wrath and to make His power known, endured with much patience vessels of wrath prepared for destruction? And He did so in order that He might make known the riches of His glory upon vessels of mercy, which He prepared beforehand for glory, even us. (Rom. 9:22-24)

God is always right (Deut. 32:4). Arguing with Him always illustrates our ignorance.

LACKING COMPASSION

Compassion has always marked God. "The Lord's lovingkindnesses indeed never cease, for His compassions never fail. They are new every morning; great is Thy faithfulness" (Lam. 3:22-23). Christ modeled compassion. "And seeing the multitudes, He felt compassion for them, because they were distressed and downcast" (Matt. 9:36). Jonah is here like the forgiven man in Jesus' parable (Matt. 18:23-35). Although he had been forgiven and shown great mercy, he failed to extend the same to others around him.

To make his point, God turns Jonah's attention to the plant. Reasoning from the lesser to the greater, God says,

> You had compassion on the plant for which you did not work, and which you did not cause to grow, which came up overnight and perished overnight. And should I not have compassion on Nineveh, the great city in which there are more than 120,000 persons who do not know the difference between their right and left hand, as well as many animals? (Jonah 4:10-11)

How is your compassion capacity? Like God's or like Jonah's?

Take a moment and look up these passages. If your compassion is cold, they should warm up the heart: Matthew 13:40-42, 49-50; 24:50-51; 25:30, 41, 46; Revelation 20:11-15.

A PARTING THOUGHT

If it can happen to Jonah, it can happen to any one of us. It's not an overnight occurrence. Slowly but surely coldness replaces compassion, until a day comes when we find ourselves callously indifferent to the need of others for God's redeeming grace. Are you running from God? Silent about God? Praying only under duress? Preaching under protest? Angry with God? Confused about life? Watching instead of working? Arguing with God? Lacking compassion?

Take a careful look at your life. The best way to avoid a terminal case of "Jonah's disease" is a periodic checkup of your own soul. Early detection will save you much grief later when God judges every deed whether it be good or evil (2 Cor. 5:10).

Let's pray together that God would give us a heart for the lost like that experienced by David Brainerd.

> I care not where I live, or what hardships I go through, so that I can but gain souls to Christ. While I am asleep, I dream of these things; as soon as I awake, the first thing I think of is this great work. All my desire is the conversion of sinners, and all my hope is in God.[3]

THREE

EVE:
A Long-Shot Loser

IMAGINE LIVING IN A perfect environment with all of your needs met, able to live out your heart's desire, and only one no-no standing between you and victory. Eve faced this scene, which we would call paradise. She didn't need a four-leaf clover or a rabbit's foot. Lady Luck had nothing to do with her future. All Eve had to do was obey God.

Unexpectedly, Satan conned Eve with a diabolical hoax. She bought into his lie and instantly this sure winner became a long-shot loser. Pay close attention to what Eve teaches us about life, because the odds have been against us ever since.

HER ENEMY: REBELLION
HER WARNINGS: DOUBTING AND THEN DISBELIEVING GOD'S WORD
HER FATAL FLAW: SELF-SATISFACTION BECOMING MORE IMPORTANT THAN OBEDIENCE TO GOD

The year was 1911; the country, England. A lawyer named Charles Dawson pursued his favorite hobby, fossil hunting, in a quarry near his home. He made what he believed to be some significant discoveries. It was near the village of Piltdown close to

EVE: A LONG-SHOT LOSER

Sussex, England, that he unearthed fragments of a fossilized skull. In his excitement, he contacted the British Museum and asked if someone might come down and verify his findings.

Arthur Woodward, who was keeper of the Department of Geology at the British Museum, responded. A year later, in 1912, the skull was displayed in the British Museum as a 500,000-year-old relic named the Neonthropas Dawsoni or Dawson's Dawn Man, named after its discoverer. Many scientists at the time questioned its authenticity, but the British Museum continually and proudly displayed the skull as the first known ancient fossil of man found in Britain.

Thirty-seven years passed until Kenneth Oakley, a scientist at the Museum, decided to reopen the investigation of the Piltdown man and the alleged fossilized skull. Through a series of chemical analyses that were impossible to do in the early part of the century, he discovered that the Piltdown man was, in fact, a rather ancient upper portion of a human skull that had been skillfully and cleverly pieced together with the jawbone of a modern ape. In a moment of time, through scientific inquiry, one of the then most highly reputed evidences for the evolution of man vanished into thin air as nothing but a hoax that had been perpetrated upon the scientific community by the scientist Dawson.

Oakley published his report in 1953, to the horror of the scientific community and the British government. In part it read like this, "From the evidence which we have obtained, it is now clear that the distinguished paleontologists and archeologists who took part in the excavations at Piltdown, were the victims of a most elaborate and carefully planned hoax."[1]

So it is also in our world that we are deceived. It has always been that way through the ages. The Bible is not without its hoaxes. In Genesis 27 we read of Jacob, who fooled his father, Isaac, into giving him the blessing instead of his older brother, Esau. In Genesis 34, Simeon and Levi tricked the residents in Shechem into being circumcised so that their sister could marry into that society, only to later slay the men in their distress. Tamar tricked her father-in-law, Judah, into believing that she was a roadside prostitute, and he lay with her (Gen. 38).

However, the greatest hoax known in all of human history, that which has had the most devastating effect upon the human race, is found in Genesis 3. There Satan, the master of deceit, conned Eve into thinking and then acting independently of God. Our first parents, Adam and Eve, were victimized by the devil's trickery, and we continue to suffer the consequences. Genesis 3:1-7 tells us all about it.

Someone has observed, "Old error in new dress is ever error none the less." Today there is a great movement among thanatologists (those who study death) to dust off and dress up the old lie of Satan, "You surely shall not die." They tell our society that beyond the horizon we call life is life on another plane, life in another dimension, regardless of where you stand with Jesus Christ.

It is opening night at Satan's playhouse in Genesis 3. We want to expose Satan's premier scheme when he attempts to poison Eve's mind with lies about God and God's Word.

DISGUISE

In Genesis 3:1 Satan arrived disguised as a serpent. "Now the serpent was more crafty than any beast of the field which the Lord God had made." The word *crafty* can be used in a positive sense or it can be used negatively. From the context, it is used in a negative sense. The same word is used in Joshua 9:4 of the Gibeonites, crafty people, who tricked Joshua and the leadership of Israel. In the same way Satan came disguised as a serpent to Eve.

Why did the serpent talk to the woman saying, "Indeed hath God said . . . ?" Why didn't he talk to Adam or to them both as a couple? He attempted to put a wedge between husband and wife to conquer by dividing, thus to capture their minds and cause them to act in disobedience to the Word of God. That's why God puts such a high premium on the oneness of husband and wife and why, as husbands and wives, we need to encourage one another, edify one another, and build up one another. The minute Satan's wedge is in, we are candidates to be chewed up by Satan and spit out in little pieces (1 Peter 5:8).

EVE: A LONG-SHOT LOSER

DOUBT

Satan says to the woman, "Indeed, has God said, 'You shall not eat from any tree of the garden'?" At first glance it seems like an innocent, religious discussion. It sounds like something the guys at a seminary would bounce around. But remember with whom she dialogues. As Shakespeare said in *King Lear,* "The prince of darkness is a gentleman." Satan is out to deceive. If he needs to, he will show up in his After Six dinnerwear. If he needs to, he will preach with the best of the King's English—all to deceive and cause us to fall by the wayside.

Satan says, in effect, "Just one question, Eve. I just want to make sure I have it right. Indeed, did God really say you shall not eat from any tree of the garden?" I'm sure Eve, like any good follower of God, welled up with pride and said, "I know exactly what God said." What she did not know at this point in time is that she was doing battle with the greatest guerrilla fighter that the world has ever known. Mao, Ho Chi Min, Castro, and Gaddafi together could not match Satan.

By the end of 3:1, Satan had used three tactics on Eve that later proved to be fatal. First, he divided in order to conquer. He did not take Adam and Eve on as a husband and wife. He singled out Eve, and he entered into an apparently innocent dialogue with her. It points out to us the value of mutual accountability.

Second, he surprised Eve with an unscheduled and obviously spectacular garden encounter. That is, he did something that was so surprising and unexpected that it threw her off balance. Eve at this moment was not practicing the presence of God, for had she been, she surely would have understood the danger.

Third, he made an apparently innocent inquiry. He came appearing as a friend in need; he just needed to know what God had said.

The Hebrew construction suggests that the question he asked was not a question of research, but rather a question of ridicule. It might better be phrased, "Is it really true that God has said . . . ?" The *New International Version* captures it best. "Did God really say you must not eat from any tree in the garden?" A modern-day paraphrase would be, "You've got to be kidding, Eve. God didn't *really* say you can't eat from any tree in the garden, did He?"

Surely Eve was shocked. She wasn't with her husband. She was surprised and knocked off balance. How in the world should she answer? I'm sure one of the things that she mulled over in her mind was, "What did God originally say?"

DIALOGUE

For us, the question is easy to answer, because it's recorded in Genesis 2:16-17. God didn't say that they couldn't eat from any tree in the garden. As a matter of fact, God created a perfect environment for them to live in; everything was absolutely perfect.

In Genesis 2:17 God says, "You shall surely die." But Eve reports, "lest you die" (3:3). She has really begun in her own mind to question the certainty of death and judgment by her paraphrase of God's original words. You can see the masterful stroke of Satan, who planted a seed of doubt and has now watched Eve cultivate it. In a moment it will become a blatant denial of the truthfulness, applicability, and personalness of the Word of God.

DENIAL

In 3:4-5 Satan feeds Eve five lies disguised by partial truth. In two sentences he fed her five pieces of spiritual poison. He tells her she will not die; God's Word is unreliable; she will be like God; God wishes to exclusively maintain His uniqueness rather than protect her from sinlessness. Satan is saying to Eve, "God is in this thing for what He can get out of it rather than what you can gain from it." The fifth lie is Satan's conveying to Eve, "I have your best interest at heart, believe me, not God. I'm more concerned for your welfare than even God is."

Many dear saints have followed the experience of Eve. I dare say some of you have walked that path. Doubt came into your life. You thought about it long enough and doubt turned into denial.

The first lie claimed that Eve would not die. In the Hebrew text Satan makes a very emphatic denial of death as a result of eating from the forbidden tree. The truth of the matter is that they did eat but did not die immediately in a physical sense. However, they did die immediately in their relationship with God. *Death* means separation. Adam and Eve thought only in the physical realm. Nonetheless, when they ate, they were spiritually separated from God by their sin. That separation led them to their later physical death.

The second lie can be inferred from Genesis 3:4. If God said they would die, but they wouldn't, then God's Word is unreliable. If it is unreliable, then there is no good reason to believe or live by it. With doubt rapidly translating into denial, Eve moved decisively to abandon the authority of God's Word. In so doing, she changed not only the course of her life and her family, but also that of the whole human race.

I'll never forget reading the biography of one of the great preachers of our century. It told of his years as a young man seriously contemplating preaching and teaching the Word of God and pastoring a church in England. But he lived in an age of liberalism and skepticism. He lived in an age when everything was doubted, so he discovered that the longer he read that literature, the more doubts crept into his mind. He began to ask questions like, Is the Word of God really true? Is it really authoritative?

Finally, he came to a point where he lost all of his assurance about the Word of God, and when he did, he cancelled all of his preaching assignments. Taking all of his books, he threw them away and went out of his house and down the street to a book shop and he bought himself a brand new Bible. He said to himself, "I'm no longer sure that this is what my father claims it to be, the Word of God. But of this I am sure. If it be the Word of God and if I come to it with an unprejudiced and open mind, it will bring assurance to my soul of itself."

Later on G. Campbell Morgan said, "That Bible found me." Some of you are old enough to remember the days of G. Campbell Morgan. The date of that incident in his life was 1887, and fifty years later, in 1938, he had become known as the prince of preachers in both Europe and the United States. A man who at one time allowed the doubts of the world to creep into his mind, who lost all of his assurance in the Word of God. But having put aside all of the books written by man and coming back to the one book written by God, reading it with an open heart, he was filled with a renewed assurance that God was who He claimed to be and His Word was true and authoritative. God blessed him in a most marvelous way.[2] Sad to say it wasn't true of Eve. In the midst of dialogue, doubt became a denial that shook Eve to the core.

Now we come to the third lie. "For God knows that in the day you eat from it your eyes will be opened, and you will be like God, knowing good and evil" (Gen. 3:5). If you look at 3:22, it says, "The Lord God said, 'Behold, the man has become like one of Us, knowing good and evil.' " It was just as Satan said. God continues, " 'And now, lest he stretch out his hand, and take also from the tree of life, and eat, and live forever'—therefore the Lord God sent him out from the garden of Eden, to cultivate the ground from which he was taken" (3:22-23).

Most of what Satan said was true, but he left out one important fact. Adam and Eve were not unchangeably holy in nature like God. Rather they were susceptible to sin if disobedience was a part of their life. They disobeyed and ate of the fruit. They sinned and God judged. They were cursed along with the serpent and the world. Ever since then, all of humanity has been cursed with sin. We have fallen from the grace of God. We have been separated from God and are in need of a Saviour.

The ultimate intent of Satan's lie was to humanize God and deify man, to say that God can become like man and man can become like God. That lie still exists in many cults today.

We find the fourth lie in verse 5. "For God knows that in the day you eat from it your eyes will be opened, and you will be like God, knowing good and evil." Satan tried to pry the mind of Eve open with the thought that God wishes to jealously maintain His uniqueness, that He wants to maintain His uniqueness of deity and does not want to share it with anyone. Satan implies that this is bad, not good. Further, God is not really protecting man's sinlessness by His prohibition; He is rather protecting His deity.

There is a fifth lie. In all five, Satan has woven together an immense assault to pummel Eve with the thought that God's

Word is untrue and unreliable; therefore, she ought to follow the desires of her own heart rather than the dictates of God's Word. This fifth untruth proves to be the lie among lies. "I, Satan, have your best interests at heart. Believe me, not God." That is the bottom line in this discussion.

Satan really hit Eve over the head, didn't he? Just boom, boom, boom. One lie after another. He knows that she is alone. He knows that she is intimidated; he knows that seeds of doubt have been planted in her mind. Now he comes in with the blow of denial. Eve must have wondered, "Who is right? This one who says God is wrong or God? How can I find the truth?"

DELIBERATION

The scientific method did not originate in the nineteenth century. It did not originate with the Industrial Revolution but rather in Genesis 3 when Eve concluded the only way she could decide whether God was right or wrong was to test Him with her own mind and senses.

Paul put it this way in Romans 1:25, speaking of those who would follow the path of Eve and then Adam. "For they exchanged the truth of God for a lie, and worshiped and served the creature rather than the Creator." By this time Eve has basically bought into the lies of Satan and she has believed that she now has a choice. Either she can choose to eat or she can choose to refrain. She believes that she has a personal preference. God's Word is no longer authoritative. God's Word no longer dictates what is right and what is wrong in her life. God's Word is no longer binding because all of a sudden there are some alternatives.

"When the woman saw that the tree was good for food, and that it was a delight to the eyes, and that the tree was desirable to make one wise, she took from its fruit and ate; and she gave also to her husband with her, and he ate" (3:6). Here we find the scientific method—empirical research in its very beginning. Eve decided that she would run three tests on the tree to see whether God was right or Satan was right.

So she subjected the tree to tests, the first being that of physical value. She observed the tree, and in observing she saw that it was good for food. It had nutritional value. These could have been Eve's thoughts. "Maybe Satan is right. Maybe God missed it. Maybe God was overrestrictive in preventing me from having all of the joy of life."

Based on this positive response, she ran a second test. Eve discovered that it was a delight to the eyes. Not only would it benefit her body nutritionally, but she also discovered that it had emotional or esthetic value. She looked upon it and it was a delight to the eyes. It was pleasing. It did not give her a bad sensation. To put it into twentieth-century language, she felt good about looking at the tree.

Eve wasn't satisfied yet. She was a good scientist. She perhaps thought, "I'll take it one step further." Then there was a third test. She looked and saw that the tree was desirable to make one wise. It had intellectual value. It would make her wise like God.

Here is what we need to learn from Genesis 3. True God-given wisdom never comes from experimenting with evil. We don't need to discover if premarital sex is bad. All we need to do is come to the Word of God, which says that God's will for us is to be sanctified, that we abstain from immorality (1 Thes. 4:3).

In the midst of Eve's deliberation, she tests God. She saw that the tree really was good. It met her needs physically, esthetically, and intellectually. That led to disobedience, for Eve rejected God's instructions and took from its fruit and ate. "She gave also to her husband with her, and he ate" (Gen. 3:6).

The battle in Genesis 3 was for the mind of Eve. It was to cause Eve to think contrary to the Word of God. When she bought into wrong thinking, she bought into wrong acting, wrong responding, and wrong living. She bought into the scheme of sensualism. Its implications are incredibly important for our money-hungry, product-hungry, pleasure-seeking society.

Sensualism is the attempt to make attractiveness, desirability, and utility replace truth as our bench mark for determining God's best in life. These factors replace God's absolute truth as a personal benchmark for determining God's will.

God said, "This is best." Eve said, "I've tested it with my senses, and I think there is something else that is better. If that is what I think, that is the way I will act."

The battle is for our minds. Satan attempts to come through doubt and denial to cause us to put the Word of God aside and to test life with our own senses.

DISASTER

Watch where that line of thinking leads. "Then the eyes of both of them were opened, and they knew that they were naked; and they sewed fig leaves together and made themselves loin coverings" (3:7). Their minds were affected, and now they perceived evil. Now they knew they were naked and desired to cover their nakedness up. Before when they were naked in the garden, all was pure. It says in Genesis 2:25, "And the man and his wife were both naked and were not ashamed." Now they are naked and also ashamed.

Guilt has now entered into the world. We find it in 3:9-11. "Then the Lord God called to the man, and said to him, 'Where are you?'" It was not that God needed to know where they were because he did not know, it was just that He wanted to alert Adam that He was there. "And he said, 'I heard the sound of Thee in the garden, and I was afraid because I was naked; so I hid myself.' And he said, 'Who told you that you were naked? Have you eaten from the tree of which I commanded you not to eat?'" Evil had found them out.

There was also conflict between the man and woman. Note in Genesis 3:12-13 that they began to blame each other for the mess. The man said, "The woman whom Thou gavest to be with me, she gave me from the tree, and I ate." Then God said to the woman, "What is this you have done?" Eve responds, "It's not my fault, don't blame me, because the serpent deceived me and I ate." She experienced great guilt.

Sin is not without consequences beyond the one who sinned. That is why the Word of God makes such a big deal about holiness in the life of believers (1 Peter 1:14-16). The Word of God cites example after example of how sin, which is seemingly limited to an individual or a couple, eventually affects whole nations.

Sin is awful, not only in the sight of God, but also in its consequences for the human race. So it was in Genesis 3 when the human race passed from life into death, from exaltation to degradation, and from true worship and kinship with God to estrangement by sin.

WRAPPING IT UP

There does exist, and has from the fall of Satan, a cosmic conflict for the control of God's kingdom. All that you will ever read in *Time, Newsweek, U.S. News and World Report*, or the *Los Angeles Times* is a product of the unrighteousness of man. It is the attempt of Satan to confuse us so that we might ultimately capitulate to his side as he attempts to wrest control of the world from God.

If you don't understand that, you will never understand life. You will never understand why Eve was a long-shot loser. That is the unvarnished truth that gives understanding to the chaos of our world.

We need to understand who Satan is. He is a created being. He is a spiritual, angelic being who morally fell through the sin of pride and who is now leading an army that is in conflict with God, righteousness, and holiness. We need to understand that Satan enlisted one-third of the angels and they morally fell. You can read about it in Revelation 12:4, 7-9.

We understand that not only did Satan enlist angelic beings to his side, but in Genesis 3 he attempted to bring also the only two living human beings to his side, to rebel against God, to deny His truthfulness, and to deny His authority. We also need to understand that in order to convert Adam and Eve from God's righteous side to his own side of evil, Satan tried to alter their thinking. He knew that to alter their thinking would be to alter their behavior (Prov. 23:7). Satan employed guerrilla warfare of which he is the master.

We also understand from our passage that Satan will attempt to lure us by attractiveness, by desirability, and by utility—the lust of the flesh, the lust of the eyes, and the boastful pride of life (1 John 2:16). He will use all of that to tug us away from our absolute, steadfast, resolute commitment to the Word of God. Adam and Eve were without excuse for what they did. Did you ever think about that? They could not blame it on their environment, because it was perfect; God created it that way. They could not blame it on their heredity, because they came from God. They could not blame it on ignorance, because God had told them all they needed to know. They could not blame it on deception, because God had warned them and Adam knew better. There was no excuse; they disobeyed God and thus they fell into sin.

We also learn that God's Word is true. God does mean what He says. Scripture serves as a compass for direction in life and an anchor for protection as the storms of sin assault our soul. When sin blows our way, our greatest defense is the Word of God. God is always true to His Word both in blessing and in judgment.

I was reading not too long ago about the life of Billy Sunday, the famed evangelist of a different era. He was saved out of baseball and out of drunkenness in Chicago. Here is what Billy Sunday said about the devil and his army of demons. "If I knew that all the devils in hell and all the devils in Pittsburgh were sitting out in the pews and sneering and jeering at me, I'd shoot God's truth into their carcasses anyway, and I purpose to keep firing away at the devils until by and by they come crawling out of their holes and swear that they were never in them. But their old hides I would assay for lead and tan for chair bottoms."[3]

Let's be wise like Billy Sunday and avoid being foolish like Eve. That way, we'll be sure winners, not long-shot losers like Eve.

FOUR

SAUL:
The "My Way" Monarch

SAUL'S PRIDE CRAVED THE Burger King approach to life—"Have it your way." His appetite for preeminence grew to the point that even God's way did not satisfy him. Saul demanded top billing. He reset time schedules to avoid waiting; he rewrote commands from headquarters to carry out what he thought was a better plan. He reacted negatively in order to recover the nation's attention when someone else received recognition.

Through it all, Saul discovered that his last-place finish resulted from his failed attempts to be first. His personal faults contributed to his fall.

HIS ENEMY: "SELF-CENTERED" APPROACH TO LIFE
HIS WARNINGS: PREOCCUPATION WITH BEING FIRST IN EVERYTHING
HIS FATAL BLOW: DISOBEYING GOD BECAUSE HE THOUGHT HE HAD A BETTER PLAN

Shortly after our daughter Lee turned three she asked her first theological question. "When Saul died, did he go to heaven or hell?" My wife immediately deferred to Dad, then a student at

SAUL: THE "MY WAY" MONARCH

Grace Theological Seminary. It's been years since then and I have forgotten exactly how I answered. It was a tough question then and still is today. I find it hard to believe that Israel's first king did not have a right relationship with God. Yet there is little in his life to demonstrate the reality of salvation.

If truth is stranger than fiction, then the account of Saul in the Bible is certainly true. Saul lived in an era when God reigned as King over Israel, yet Saul himself later ruled. He had all of the requisite outward attributes but was inwardly weak. He started in glory and finished in shame. He conquered the Philistines but could not conquer himself. He ruled Israel, yet possessed bitter jealously toward a young teen in his kingdom. He sought after God for wisdom but is best known for seeking Samuel through the witch of En-dor in defiance of God's will. What began with promise of success fizzled at the end in failure. First Chronicles 10:13-14 provides God's commentary on Saul's life.

> Saul died for his trespass which he committed against the Lord, because of the word of the Lord which he did not keep; and also because he asked counsel of a medium, making inquiry of it, and did not inquire of the Lord. Therefore He killed him, and turned the kingdom to David the son of Jesse.

How could this happen? It certainly did not start that way.

BACKGROUND

Two sins paved the way for Saul to become king of Israel. First, there was the failure of Samuel to raise a godly seed.

> And it came about when Samuel was old that he appointed his sons judges over Israel.... His sons, however, did not walk in his ways, but turned aside after dishonest gain and took bribes and perverted justice. (1 Sam. 8:1, 3)

Second, because of Israel's dissatisfaction with Samuel's dishonest sons, they demanded a king like the other nations. "Now appoint a king for us to judge us like all the nations" (1 Sam. 8:5).

This violated God's will. "Moreover, you shall not follow the customs of the nation which I shall drive out before you, for they did all these things, and therefore I have abhorred them" (Lev. 20:23). In asking for a king, they rejected God from being King over them (1 Sam. 8:7).

God, through Samuel, warned the nation that there would be severe implications if a human king replaced Him as their ruler. The king would take their sons and daughters as slaves; the king would take their best fields, vineyards, and seed (1 Sam. 8:14-15); and the king would take slaves and Israel's flocks for himself (1 Sam. 8:11-17). But the nation refused to listen. So badly did they want a king to judge and defend them like the other nations that God finally condescended to let them have their own way (1 Sam. 8:19-22). Little did they know that God would select a king whose heart mirrored their own.

At this point the spotlight turned to Saul the son of Kish, a Benjamite. Outwardly he seemed to be the ideal selection. Not only was he choice and handsome, but he was a head and shoulders taller than any of the people (1 Sam. 9:2).

Samuel, in obedience to God's command, anointed Saul as Israel's first human king (1 Sam. 10:1). Samuel then called the nations together to introduce them to their new king. Although Saul shied away from God's appointment, most of the people accepted him and shouted, "Long live the king." But certain worthless men rejected him (1 Sam. 10:17-27).

To unquestionably verify Saul as king, God placed the peoples of Jabesh-gilead under siege by the Ammonites. Saul, empowered by God, brought the nation together, and they defeated the Ammonites (1 Sam. 11:1-11). Samuel called the nations together to go to Gilgal and make Saul king (1 Sam. 11:14-15).

As a final reminder, God through Samuel told the nation that they had done evil in asking for a human king (1 Sam. 12:17-18). The message is verified by the signs of thunder and rain.

They had only one option at this point—to obey God.

Now therefore, here is the king whom you have chosen, whom you

SAUL: THE "MY WAY" MONARCH

have asked for, and behold, the Lord has set a king over you. If you will fear the Lord and serve Him, and listen to His voice and not rebel against the command of the Lord, then both you and also the king who reigns over you will follow the Lord your God. And if you will not listen to the voice of the Lord, but rebel against the command of the Lord, then the hand of the Lord will be against you, as it was against your fathers.... Only fear the Lord and serve Him in truth with all your heart; for consider what great things He has done for you. But if you still do wickedly, both you and your king shall be swept away." (1 Sam. 12:13-15, 24-25)

That's how Saul, from a human perspective, replaced God as king of Israel. Although he ruled for over three decades, Saul lost the throne because he was out of character with God's will for him.

IMPATIENCE

By prior agreement, Saul was to go to Gilgal, wait for Samuel for seven days, allow Samuel to offer peace and burnt offerings, and then go to battle against the Philistines.

Saul began well. But after seven days, when Samuel did not appear, the king grew impatient. He undoubtedly would have liked to have displayed on the rear bumper of his chariot a personalized license plate like one I recently saw while driving on a California freeway: IH82W8, that is, "I hate to wait."

The "my way" monarch disregarded Samuel's instructions and offered the sacrifice himself (1 Sam. 13:8-9). As soon as Saul completed his unauthorized task, Samuel appeared. Saul undoubtedly believed he had been victimized by the military strategy of "hurry up...and wait." Another king, Uzziah, would later offer unauthorized sacrifice and be punished by God with a lifetime case of leprosy (2 Chron. 26:16-21). Saul had committed no minor blunder.

Samuel first reacted with a question, "What have you done?" Saul, knowing he had done wrong, tried to make an excuse. He tried to shift the blame to the people, Samuel, and the Philistines

(1 Sam. 13:11). Saul wanted God's blessing but he would not obey God's directions through Samuel. Samuel's indictment of Saul must have struck fear in Saul's heart.

> And Samuel said to Saul, "You have acted foolishly; you have not kept the commandment of the Lord your God, which He commanded you, for now the Lord would have established your kingdom over Israel forever. But now your kingdom shall not endure. The Lord has sought out for Himself a man after His own heart, and the Lord has appointed him as ruler over His people, because you have not kept what the Lord commanded you." (1 Sam. 13:13-14)

Saul was much like the Jews after they had been liberated from Egypt. There the people became impatient and spoke against God and Moses (Num. 21:4-5). God's timetable is usually slower than our human willingness to wait and be patient. God puts a high premium on patience. It is a part of His character (Jer. 15:15; Rom. 2:4; 1 Peter 3:20). God exercises His patience toward us in salvation (1 Tim. 1:16; 2 Peter 3:9). Patience is essential to us as believers because it is included in the fruit of God's Spirit (Gal. 5:22); a mark of true love (1 Cor. 13:4); commanded of Christians (1 Thes. 5:14; 1 Peter 2:20); essential to the worthy walk (Eph. 4:2; Col. 3:12).

We stand vulnerable to Saul's mistake. We want God's blessing in our lives, but impatiently wanting more in less time, we tend to take life into our own hands and disobey God's will. Every twentieth-century speedster needs to tuck the psalmist's commitment away in his heart to protect against those times he feels like hurrying up. "Wait for the Lord; be strong, and let your heart take courage; yes, wait for the Lord" (Ps. 27:14).

INSUBORDINATION

Saul's impatience led to disobedience. Now his impatience turns into insubordination that results in even greater condemnation by God. In 1· Samuel 15:1, the Prophet Samuel reemphasized the chain of command to Saul. "Then Samuel said to Saul, 'The Lord sent me to anoint you as king over His people, over Israel; now therefore listen to the words of the Lord' " (1 Sam. 15:1). It was the Lord who sent Samuel to Saul; the people of Israel are God's people, not Saul's. The kingship of Saul is by God's grace. The logical conclusion is that Saul needs to completely obey the will of God.

God desired to punish Amalek for the ill treatment he showed the Jews when they came up from Egypt, so He commissioned Saul to destroy the Amalekites. All men, women, children, infants, ox, sheep, camels, and donkeys were to be put to death. These orders demanded absolute, complete obedience (15:2-3). The good news is that Saul defeated the Amalekites. The bad news is that he badly disobeyed God. Insubordination marked this hollow victory.

God's instructions were clear; do not spare Agag and slaughter *all* of the animals. "But Saul and the people spared Agag and the best of the sheep, the oxen, the fatlings, the lambs, and all that was good, and were not willing to destroy them utterly; but everything despised and worthless, that they utterly destroyed" (1 Sam. 15:9).

Notice God's response. " 'I regret that I have made Saul king, for he has turned back from following Me, and has not carried out My commands.' And Samuel was distressed and cried out to the Lord all night" (1 Sam. 15:11). Now notice Saul's reaction to the victory—he set up a monument for himself and bragged of his success to Samuel (15:12-13). Saul should have let these two proverbs reign in his heart: "Pride goes before destruction" (Prov. 16:18). "Before honor comes humility" (Prov. 15:33).

Then Samuel lowered the boom. "What then is this bleating of the sheep in my ears, and the lowing of the oxen which I hear? Why then did you not obey the voice of the Lord, but rushed upon the spoil and did what was evil in the sight of the Lord?" (1 Sam. 15:14, 19) Saul had disobeyed.

No other portion of Scripture so emphasizes God's demand for total obedience. Samuel put it all in perspective with these choice words.

Has the Lord as much delight in burnt offerings and sacrifices as in obeying the voice of the Lord? Behold, to obey is better than sacrifice, and to heed than the fat of rams. For rebellion is as the sin of divination, and insubordination is as iniquity and idolatry. Because you have rejected the word of the Lord, He has also rejected you from being king. (1 Sam. 15:22-23)

This is a common theme throughout Scripture (Ps. 51:16-17; Prov. 15:8; Jer. 7:22-23; Hosea 6:6; Micah 6:6-8; 1 John 2:4-6).

Two important lessons stand out from this phase of Saul's life. First, he desired to be honored by the people as much as, if not more than, by God. In 1 Samuel 15:15 and 15:21 Saul excuses his act of disobedience by blaming it on the "the people." The unvarnished truth reveals that Saul listened to the people rather than to God and flunked one of the foundational tests of spiritual leadership. "I feared the people and listened to their voice" (15:24).

Second lesson—it is better to be honored by God for complete obedience and dishonored by the people rather than the other way around. Saul chose the people's honor over God's and lost the kingdom. Even at the end Saul sought the honor of men. "Please honor me now before the elders of my people and before Israel" (15:30). Samuel delivered the bad news for a second time—God had rejected Saul as king (15:26, 28).

God demands total obedience from his people. The Ivory soap approach of 99 44/100 percent obedient won't cut it. That's why the Lord Jesus Christ said, "Why do you call Me 'Lord, Lord,' and do not do what I say?" (Luke 6:46)

An unknown author summarizes this aspect of Saul's life well.[1]
Ye call me Master and obey me not;
Ye call me Light and see me not;
Ye call me Way and walk me not;
Ye call me Life and desire me not;
Ye call me Wise and follow me not;
Ye call me Fair and love me not;
Ye call me Rich and ask me not;
Ye call me Eternal and seek me not;
Ye call me Gracious and trust me not;

SAUL: THE "MY WAY" MONARCH

Ye call me Noble and serve me not;
Ye call me Mighty and honor me not;
Ye call me Just and fear me not;
If I condemn you BLAME ME not!

INDIGNATION

God intended to carry out his promise of removing Saul from the kingship. Samuel, commissioned by God, traveled to Jesse's house to anoint a new king (16:1). This time God would select a man who embraced His way. Saul had outwardly displayed the epitome of kingly qualities. Everyone, including Samuel, looked for similar qualities in the new candidate. God had a better plan, however.

Seven sons of Jesse passed before Samuel and God rejected them all. Why?

> But the Lord said to Samuel, "Do not look at his appearance or at the height of his stature, because I have rejected him; for God sees not as man sees, for man looks at the outward appearance, but the Lord looks at the heart." (1 Sam. 16:7)

> I have found David the son of Jesse, a man after my heart, who will do all My will. (Acts 13:22)

No human would have done it God's way. Finally, Samuel asked Jesse to call for his youngest son, David, who was tending sheep while all of this important process went on. When David arrived, "Samuel took the horn of oil and anointed him in the midst of his brothers; and the Spirit of the Lord came mightily upon David from that day forward" (1 Sam. 16:13). Concurrently, the Spirit of the Lord departed from Saul. Little did Saul know that this David would play a major role in the remainder of his rule.

David not only became a valued part of the king's court as a musician to soothe Saul (16:14-23), but he would also rescue Saul and Israel from the Philistines when the giant Goliath appeared on the scene. After slaying Goliath, David's success continued. "So David went out wherever Saul sent him, and prospered; and Saul set him over the men of war. And it was pleasing in the sight of all the people and also in the sight of Saul's servants" (1 Sam. 18:5).

David became a legend in his own time. Songs were written about his victories. One went like this: "Saul has slain his thousands, but David his ten thousands" (18:7). That song became the straw that broke Saul's emotional back. With his ego shattered, jealousy controlled Saul. From that moment on, Saul, filled with prideful indignation, tried to kill David. It is almost a classic case of paranoia, as Saul exhibited anger (18:8); suspicion (18:9); fear (18:12); and dread (18:15). He schemed to achieve David's death (18:17-30); he ordered David killed by his servants (19:1); and on several occasions he pursued David with Israel's army (24:2; 26:2). Finally, after David on two occasions refused to kill Saul when he could, Saul surrendered his pride and the fires of his indignation died down (1 Sam. 26:21).

Saul reminds me of the Greek who lost his life through envy.

> His fellow citizens had reared a statue to one of their number who was a celebrated victor in the public games. So strong was the feeling of envy which this incited in the breast of one of the hero's rivals that he went forth every night in order, if possible, to destroy that monument. After repeated efforts he moved it from its pedestal, and it fell, but in its fall it crushed him.[2]

Two simple truths could have transformed Saul from an indignant king to one marked by gratitude and dignity: "Give preference to one another in honor" (Rom. 12:10); "Render to all what is due them ... honor to whom honor" (Rom. 13:7).

IMPUDENCE

One final episode stains the reign of Saul. When he should have been old and wise, he acted foolishly, like a young man. It seemed like something an impudent teenager would do, rather than a seasoned veteran.

By this time Saul knew his rule could not last much longer, and

SAUL: THE "MY WAY" MONARCH

Samuel, his one link to God, had died (1 Sam. 28:3). When Saul inquired of the Lord, the Lord did not answer him (28:6), though he desperately wanted to hear from God. His desperation drove him to do the unthinkable—consult a human medium. This totally contradicted the will of God (Lev. 19:31).

Disguised to avoid recognition, Saul asked the woman medium at En-dor to bring up Samuel. When she objected because it was unlawful, Saul promised immunity. Samuel arrived back from the dead. In all likelihood it was by God's power, not the woman's, for she was shocked by Samuel's arrival and immediately knew that her customer was actually Saul (28:12). Samuel asks, "Why have you disturbed me by bringing me up?" (28:15)

Saul's feeble answer could be paraphrased, "I greatly fear, for I am unable to rule without God's help and instruction." That which the king took lightly before is an obvious imperative when it is no longer available.

Samuel rebukes Saul with these words,

> And Samuel said, "Why then do you ask me, since the Lord has departed from you and has become your adversary? And the Lord has done accordingly as He spoke through me; for the Lord has torn the kingdom out of your hand and given it to your neighbor, to David. As you did not obey the Lord and did not execute His fierce wrath on Amalek, so the Lord has done this thing to you this day. Moreover the Lord will also give over Israel along with you into the hands of the Philistines, therefore tomorrow you and your sons will be with me. Indeed the Lord will give over the army of Israel into the hands of the Philistines!" (1 Sam. 28:16-19)

Saul lacked only one ability to be a successful king—the ability to listen to God with the commitment to obey. Saul needed to be, and we need to be, "all ears" when God speaks.

A missionary translator was endeavoring to find a word for *obedience* in the native language. This was a virtue seldom practiced among the people into whose language he wanted to translate the New Testament. As he returned home from the village one day, he whistled for his dog and it came running at full speed. An old native, seeing this, said admiringly in the native tongue, "Your dog is all ear." Immediately the missionary knew he had his word for obedience.[3]

THE BOTTOM LINE

Saul's career as king proved to be less than illustrious. It all began with self-willed judges (1 Sam. 8:3) that provoked a self-willed people (1 Sam. 8:19-20). This led to a self-willed king (1 Sam. 13—28) whom God would later remove from the throne. The "my way" monarch met his end on the battlefield. As God had warned, Saul died in defeat (1 Sam. 28:19; 31:1-6).

God often teaches us by paradox what at first seems contradictory to common knowledge but in fact later proves to be true. That is why Paul admonishes the Colossians to set their minds on the things above, not on the things that are on the earth (Col. 3:2). No two kings are more paradoxical by comparison than Israel's first human king, Saul, and their last king, the Lord Jesus Christ.

First, the people craved Saul as their king (1 Sam. 8:19-20). But the people rejected Christ when He came to rule (Matt. 27:20-25; John 6:66). It is not human reason but divine wisdom we need when establishing spiritual leadership.

Next, Saul was impatient and insubordinate because he thought his plans were better than God's (1 Sam. 13, 15). Christ, on the other hand, made God's will His will (Matt. 26:39; John 4:34; 6:38). He also patiently waited for his hour as predetermined by His Father (John 2:4; 7:30; 8:20). God's way always proves best.

Finally, Saul loved the top spot but ended up a loser (1 Sam. 31). In contrast, Christ was willing to be last and thus God made Him ruler over all (2 Cor. 8:9; Phil. 2:5-11).

> It is not so among you, but whoever wishes to become great among you shall be your servant, and whoever wishes to be first among you shall be your slave; just as the Son of Man did not come to be served, but to serve, and to give His life a ransom for many. (Matt. 20:26-28)

PART TWO

HOPE: SOME FELL BUT RECOVERED WHILE FIGHTING

FIVE

ELIJAH:
The Lone Prophet

BECAUSE LONDONERS FEARED THE nightly World War II air raids by Nazi Germany, a pastor posted this instructive note outside his church to encourage the frightened wartime residents. "If your knees knock, kneel on them."

In our study Elijah received a "bomb" from Jezebel. Instead of kneeling to stop his knee-knock, he runs to seek relief. Fear dressed Elijah's mind in a straightjacket called "the lone prophet complex." Let's look at God's prognosis and prescription for this emotional crippler. Elijah's painful attempt to escape from reality revolves around these basic elements in a segment of his life.

HIS ENEMY: FATIGUE THAT LED TO FEAR OF PEOPLE AND CIRCUMSTANCES

HIS MISTAKE: SHOULDERING MORE RESPONSIBILITY FOR A LONGER PERIOD OF TIME THAN GOD INTENDED LED TO PHYSICAL AND SPIRITUAL BREAKDOWN

HIS RECOVERY: THROUGH REST, RECONSTITUTION, AND REMEMBRANCE THERE IS RESTORATION TO CONFIDENT LIVING

John Bunyan, a seventeenth-century Puritan preacher, wrote

the most frequently read piece of Christian literature outside of the Bible, *Pilgrim's Progress*. It's about a Christian named Pilgrim who encounters all sorts of dangers as he trudges through life. Pilgrim stumbles into the "slough of despond" and he is almost caught in the "flatterer's net," but he always progresses.

It dawned on me that if someone were to write a comparable book today, it probably would be very different. Instead of picturing a humble pilgrim hiking his way through a hazardous foreign land, it would most likely describe "Supersaint's Successes." It would be the Walt Disney version of the Christian life.

Chuck Swindoll, in his excellent book *Three Steps Forward, Two Steps Back*, reflects on this kind of Pollyanna Christianity.[1] He humorously describes its creed as "the four spiritual flaws." Number 1: Because you are a Christian, all your problems are automatically, immediately solved. Number 2: All the problems you will ever have, in their smallest detail, are addressed in the Bible. Number 3: If you're having problems, you're unspiritual. Number 4: Being exposed to sound Bible teaching automatically solves all problems.

Supersaint might face fairy-tale fantasies, but John Bunyan's book more accurately portrays the battle life brings our way. The only thing gained from following "the four spiritual flaws" is a guilt trip, and neither you nor I can afford such cruel travel.

If we turn to 1 Kings 19 we'll abruptly and painfully bump into one of God's great prophets on an off day. Elijah would have identified with Pilgrim. He knew the ecstasy of success and he knew the agony of stumbling. I think you'll be able to quickly identify with Elijah. Elijah was a great man of God, but he fell.

I hope your heart will be encouraged as we see God's cure for a spiritual disease that strikes many Christians. Read carefully, because one day it might come your way and you'll need to learn from the life of Elijah.

THE CHARACTERS

It might be good if we pause for just a minute to find out who the people involved in this story are. Ahab is king of Israel, the ten

ELIJAH: THE LONE PROPHET

northern tribes of the Divided Kingdom. Ahab is distinguished not by his sanctity but by his sinfulness. Ahab also made the Asherah, a wooden symbol of a female deity, and thus he did more to provoke the Lord God of Israel than all of the kings who were before him (1 Kings 16:30-33).

Ahab was a weak man married to a wicked woman. Her name was Jezebel. Jezebel, daughter of the king of Sidon, was the spiritual leader in the home; she took Ahab in her spiritual slipstream to worship many of the idolatrous pagan gods and goddesses in the ancient near east.

Jezebel had an unhealthy dominance over Ahab. This is one of the more pointed examples of spiritual disaster in the home when a woman takes the lead and violently usurps it from her husband. Having control of Ahab, she had control of the nation of Israel and she led it into utter disaster. So it was to both Ahab and Jezebel that God sent a marvelous prophet named Elijah.

You may remember Elijah as the instigator of a three-year drought in Israel that infuriated Ahab (1 Kings 17:1). Elijah was the man who humbled the dead idols of the ancient Near East. In a moment of power he called fire down from heaven and proved unquestionably that there was only one true living God (1 Kings 18). He was the prophet who ordered 450 prophets of Baal and 400 prophets of the Asherah to die at the hands of the Israelites (1 Kings 18:40). He was the prophet who prayed seven times to heaven, "God, rain upon the land," after which a storm supernaturally blew in from the Mediterranean and drenched the parched land (18:45).

The time was about 860 B.C. It was a little over 100 years since the kingdom had divided through Solomon's sinfulness and about 120 years before God would send Assyria to take the northern ten tribes captive. Elijah had seemingly conquered Ahab and Jezebel. Unquestionably he had proven that the Lord God was the living God. With her prophets dead, Jezebel was fresh with the news of her spiritual defeat. In an angry rage that would vie with a tornado for fury, Jezebel sent a messenger to Elijah, "saying, 'So may the gods do to me and even more, if I do not make your life as the life of one of them by tomorrow about this time'" (1 Kings 19:2).

63

Elijah had already made the twelve-mile dash from Mt. Carmel to Jezreel, the capital city where Ahab and Jezebel resided. I believe Elijah made that trip to wait for the abdication of Ahab and Jezebel because the proof of God's reality had been so conclusive. But unbeknownst to Elijah, Ahab and Jezebel were not down for the count. She sent a never-to-be-forgotten "nasty gram" which had an incredible effect upon Elijah.

In a moment of time Elijah was shocked by a paralyzing emotion that caused him to react in a way that went against the very grain of his courageous nature—he feared. One writer has described the bug that bit Elijah this way:

> Fear is a phantom giant. Drifting in through cracks in the floorboards or filtering down like a chilling mist, the fog called fear whispers omens of the unknown and the unseen. Surrounding individuals in its binding, billowing robe, the creature hisses, "What if? What if?" One blast of its awful breath transforms saints into atheists reversing a person's entire mind-set. Its bite releases a paralyzing venom in its victim and it isn't long before doubt begins to dull vision. To one who falls prey to this attack, the creature displays no mercy. It falls full weight on its back and laughs with glee at its crippled plaything and circles for another savage assault. Lurking in the shadows around every imaginable corner it threatens to poison your inner peace and outer poise. Bully that it is, the creature relies on scare tactics and surprise attacks. It watches for your vulnerable moment then picks the lock that safeguards your security. Once inside, it strikes quickly to transform spiritual muscle into mental mush. And the prognosis for recovery is neither bright nor cheery.[2]

Recognize it? Of all the emotions that God has put into us, I personally have done more battle with fear than all of them put together. The dictionary defines fear as a painful emotion caused by the apprehension of evil and marked by the desire to flee or to avoid it. It has reached epidemic proportions for those of us who live in what experts have tagged the "age of anxiety."

Elijah was not the only prophet to face similar circumstances. Jeremiah had faithfully preached the message of God. He had not compromised at all, but the people were not appreciative, and they schemed to have him killed (Jer. 11:18-20). In Acts 7 we read about Stephen's first public preaching assignment. When it was over, the audience was so enraged by his message that they took up stones and killed him. Chrysostom, who was known as the golden-mouthed orator of the fourth century A.D., received a threat similar to that of Elijah from another woman, the empress Eudoxia, to which he replied, "Go tell her I fear nothing but sin itself." What a great response to a person, group, or nation that would threaten to shut the mouth of God through His redeemed!

FEAR'S CAUSE

Until Jezebel's messenger arrived, sin was all Elijah had feared. But in a microsecond, he had a distorted life view. He no longer saw life from God's perspective. Until that moment, Elijah had trusted God for the incredible and the impossible. He had trusted God to shut the heavens to rain no more on the land. He had trusted God to supply his food through ravens. He had trusted God to be supported in the land by a widow who had no support. He had trusted God to conceal and protect him from Ahab for three and a half years. He had trusted God to prove Himself to be true and to defeat 850 pagan prophets. He trusted God when he prayed for rain.

The response of fear in such men as Elijah makes the statements about fear that have been offered by other men very real. Henry David Thoreau wrote, "Nothing is so much to be feared as fear." In a very deep time of need in our own country, Franklin Delano Roosevelt said, "The only thing we have to fear is fear itself." Elijah would have done well to remember what David had written earlier, "I sought the Lord, and He answered me, and delivered me from all my fears" (Ps. 34:4). In Proverbs we read, "The fear of man brings a snare, but he who trusts in the Lord will be exalted" (Prov. 29:25).

Why did Elijah run? He was faithful, he had seemed invincible, he had been used powerfully in the hand of Almighty God; but his picture of God had lost its perception of power. His distorted view catapulted him on a roller-coaster ride that he would not soon forget.

FEAR'S CONSEQUENCE

Elijah arose and ran over 100 miles from Jezreel south to Beersheba. There he left his servant, marched resolutely into the desert, and when the strain of travel became too great, sat down under a juniper tree, sometimes called a "broom bush" (1 Kings 19:3-4).

Let me tell you what a broom bush is. If you took a ten-foot tall mop, starched it, and put it in the ground handle down, letting the mop flop out, you would have a good imitation of a broom bush. It was the foliage in the desert that was most sought by a weary traveler because of the extended shade that it offered.

Finding temporary and immediate relief, he looked to heaven and said, "Lord, take my life, I no longer desire to live." Elijah wasn't the first person to despair of his life. Job asked God for death because he despaired of his painful physical afflictions (Job 6:8-9). Jonah despaired of life because he disagreed with God—a losing cause every time (Jonah 4:3). Moses despaired of his life and said, "Lord, take it now" (Num. 11:10-15). The burden of leading rebellious Israel had become too great, and he buckled under the load that he couldn't carry by himself. Jeremiah regretted his life because he could no longer bear the exceeding sinfulness of the nation (Jer. 20:14-18). What Elijah and the others had forgotten, and what we need to be reminded of, is that God and God alone is the giver and the taker of life (Deut. 32:39).

Have you ever asked God to take you out of the race? That's where Elijah was.

FEAR'S CURE

Elijah's distorted life view produced a disobedient life response. He ran from the task, he was fearful of a woman instead of fearing Almighty God, and then he asked what God Himself had not dared to do, "Take my life." God might have said, "Elijah, you know what I've done in the past. In a moment of stupidity and idiocy you've run and ruined the whole program." But that wasn't how the Lord dealt with Elijah.

There's probably no better biblical outline of the very practical methodology of counseling than we see here as Elijah comes to the counseling couch of the living God. God would meet Elijah's need and restore him so that he could continue to serve. The cure involved taking a *detour from life's normal course*. The first step that Elijah needed to take was physical rest (1 Kings 19:5). Elijah, having run and having gone out into the desert, is now sleeping under this broom bush. The last three and a half years have been tough—no vacation, no time out, and no time off. His gas tank was dry. His emotional reserve tank was empty. Physical exhaustion had set in.

I would be quick to add that physical exhaustion is not always the cause of fear. But frequently when the cause of fear is circumstances rather than from a neurological or physiological reason, then fatigue makes life seem worse. God knew Elijah's real need to lie down and rest.

The second step was reconstitution of his body (19:5-8). "Behold, there was an angel touching him, and he said to him, 'Arise and eat.' " This was the original continental breakfast. Elijah is the only man in the Bible who was served breakfast in bed by an angel. What did he eat? In his hand was the only dish that was on the menu—a bread cake baked on hot stones. It would have been the Palestinian version of a tortilla cooked on a hot stone.

Elijah took God's advice. Whether he wanted to or not, he ate, drank, and lay down again. Then the angel of the Lord came a second time. Note that the physical exhaustion that plagued Elijah was not cured by a quick nap or an hour out of the race. Elijah was out of the race not for days but for months. He slept and he ate; he slept and he ate; he slept and he ate, and then the angel said, "Arise and eat because the journey is too great for you." Regain your strength, Elijah, there is much to be done in the recovery process. He finally arose, ate, drank, and went in the strength of that food.

God had prepared him to take the next step. He had come 100 miles from Jezreel to Beersheba, plus another day's journey into the wilderness. Now, over a forty-day period he would travel more than 200 miles from Beersheba south to Sinai and come to the foot of Horeb, the mount of God. Elijah took forty days and forty nights to arrive there, probably at a pace of five miles a day. At a normal rate you can walk a mile about every twenty minutes. If Elijah took a twenty-minute break at the two-and-a-half-mile mark, he walked for two hours and he rested for twenty-two hours every day. That schedule lasted until he reached Horeb.

At that point, the rest and reconstitution process had gained enough for Elijah's mind to recover. Then God did something significant—it's the third step of the cure—He brought a reminder of the power and the presence of God to Elijah (19:9-14). God sent him to the mountain that had been the scene of great wonders in the days past. Horeb, also called Mt. Sinai, stood as a colossal monument to God's power. At this mountain Moses met God in the burning bush which was not consumed and talked with the voice of Almighty God (Ex. 3). This was the place where God gave to Moses His levitical legislation, the Ten Commandments. At this mountain the nation saw the power of God come down in fire and wind and earthquake (Ex. 19).

As Elijah walked, the mountain was always on the horizon, and the longer he traveled, the closer it got and the bigger it became until one day he stood at its foot. "He came there to a cave, and lodged there; and behold, the Word of the Lord came to him" (1 Kings 19:9).

Mindful again that this is a classic illustration on counseling technique, watch what God does. God does not ask him a question in order to learn facts. God already knew what Elijah's problem was. Nevertheless, He asks, "What in the world are you doing here?" Now that's a loose paraphrase of what the Hebrew text says. It is always good to let the counselee make a statement, and that's what God did. Elijah responded, "I have been very zealous for the Lord, the God of hosts; for the sons of Israel have forsaken Thy covenant, torn down thine altars and killed Thy prophets with the sword. And I alone am left; and they seek my life, to take it away" (v. 10).

Poor Elijah. You know, Elijah did not catch the "lone prophet complex" the day he arrived in Jezreel at the end of that twelve-mile dash hoping the king and queen would abdicate. It was earlier. Look back to 1 Kings 18:22. Elijah is in the midst of challenging the prophets of Baal and the Asherah. He says to the people, "I alone am left a prophet of the Lord, but Baal's prophets are 450 men." Elijah was wrong on all counts. There were not only 450 prophets of Baal, but there were 400 prophets of the Asherah and at least another 400 that we don't even see that come on the scene in 1 Kings 22:6. And neither was Elijah the lone, true prophet of God. When Jezebel destroyed the prophets of the Lord, Obadiah, the servant of Ahab, took 100 prophets and hid them by fifties in a cave and provided them with bread and water (1 Kings 18:4).

Elijah's body had been rested and it was now reconstituted. But his mind needed to be reoriented to the things of God. He needed a trip down memory lane, so God made the travel arrangements. God said to Elijah, "Go forth, and stand on the mountain before the Lord" (19:11). And before Elijah could move one foot in front of the other to walk out of his cave, the Lord was passing by. A great wind was rending the mountain and breaking it into pieces of rock before the Lord. But the Lord was not in it. After the wind an earthquake, but the Lord was not in the earthquake. And after the earthquake a fire, but the Lord was not in the fire either. Where was God? How come wind, earthquake, fire? The answer is very simple. All three declare the power of God.

What is God trying to tell Elijah? Simply this. "Elijah, I'm not in the midst of it. What I want you to actually see is My power to judge. Elijah, I don't care what Jezebel wrote. I don't care what she said. I don't care what she's done in the past or what she'll do in the future. Be reminded that I am a God of great power, and I can snuff them out right now if I want to."

Afterward, Ahab did send men, three groups of fifty each, with a message for Elijah. Do you know what happened to the first two groups of men? They died in flames of fire that came down from heaven—they immediately expired (2 Kings 1:9-14). The third group was so afraid of God that God allowed them to live.

Later on, as recorded in 1 Kings 22:34-35, God takes Ahab's life by an arrow fired at random by a Syrian archer in the field of battle and providentially guided by God's homing radar right to the heart of Ahab. Jezebel was thrown to her death from a balcony, and trampled underfoot by Jehu, then the king of Israel (2 Kings 9:33). And later, as Elijah had prophecied, her body was eaten by dogs. Ahab and Jezebel were no contest—none whatsoever.

In contrast to the great wind came the sound of a gentle breeze, or as the Hebrew text expresses it, "a small, quiet voice." I believe this represents the tender mercy and gracious nature of Almighty God, who wants to see Elijah restored to health and then restored to prophetship in Israel.

Elijah emerged from his protective cave having heard the sound, wrapped his face in his mantel, and stood at the entrance of the cave. A voice then came to him; God asked the same question He had asked before the wind, the earthquake, and the fire. "What are you doing here, Elijah?" It almost sounds like an echo, doesn't it? Elijah, like a windup doll, answers in the same way he had before.

It's difficult to counsel over the telephone or through another person. You can't see their face; you can't watch their eyes; you can't hear the tone of their voice. And there was something different about Elijah; although his words were the same, his mind-set was totally different. After rest, after restoration, and after remembrance, Elijah was ready to acknowledge his error, to abandon his way, and to again embrace life with God at the helm.

In the final step, God restores Elijah to the service from which he had run (19:15-18). God gives Elijah three tasks. But look carefully at verse 18—God gave Himself an assignment too, so they would be co-laborers in the work. God says, "Yet I will leave 7,000 in Israel, all the knees that have not bowed to Baal and every mouth that has not kissed him."

Interesting, isn't it? God's message is, "Elijah, you go and you do your part, and I'll go and do My part. And you know what, Elijah? Life's going to go on; it's not over."

Elijah left there with absolute confidence that God was equal to the task and with absolute confidence that God's power, which had been manifested through him before, would be manifested through him again. His body had been rested, and it found reconstitution in the proper diet. His mind received a healthy dose of remembering God's power. God now restores him to service. But it's not the end of the story for us. Elijah lived some 2,900 years ago. You and I live in a time that is fast approaching the twenty-first century. The ultimate question in all of this is, "What does it mean to us?"

LESSONS TO LEARN

Here are some final thoughts that will wrap up all that we've seen in the life of Elijah. When fear comes and we feel its stinging bite, we will know the cure. We can reach for the antidote, take it, and know that what God did for Elijah He can also do for us.

Victory breeds vulnerability. When Elijah had reached the apex of his ministry and had unquestionably downed the prophets of Baal and Asherah and had then gone back to Jezreel expecting an abdication, he was met with a message from Jezebel that launched him on his run for life. When we are on the top, it's just the time that Satan wants to strike, to strike quickly and cut us down with fear.

The best of us are vulnerable. There's no such thing as immunity from the onslaughts of Satan, no matter who you are, what your background is, where you've been, or what you've done. Elijah is proof positive. Elijah was a man just like us, according to James 5:17. The Greek text literally says, "He was a man of similar pathos." He had the same emotional makeup as we have. If he feared and ran, then we have that same capacity. We, like Elijah, are subject to stumbling.

The fear we've been talking about has been generated from reaction to circumstances outside of our control—fearful responses that have found their breeding ground in a body fatigued and tired. Elijah's fear was generated by a distorted view of life because he had forgotten to see the fullness of God's glory. But it's curable. If you suffer the same problem as Elijah, there's hope for you. The cure involves taking a detour from the progress of life—as did Elijah. Call time out in the press of life and take a very close look at God. You need rest and reconstitution.

Supernatural courage will be born out of our intense concentration on the power of God. It's the kind of courage that sustained Elijah when God told him to get up and return to the battle. It's the confidence David spoke of in Psalm 56:3-4: "When I am afraid, I will put my trust in Thee. In God, whose word I praise, in God I have put my trust; I will not be afraid. What can mere man do to me?"

The good news is that renewed courage worked for David. It worked for Elijah. It worked for the great English statesman, William Gladstone, who, on being questioned about the secret of his unusual serenity, replied, "At the foot of my bed where I can see it on retiring and on arising in the morning are the words, 'God shalt keep him in perfect peace whose mind is stayed on Thee because he trusts in Thee' " (Isa. 26:3).

And, it will work for you. "For God has not given us a spirit of timidity, but of power and love and discipline" (2 Tim. 1:7).

SIX

SAMSON:
The Wayward Warrior

MR. & MRS. MANOAH'S firstborn son arrived as Israel's promised deliverer. He qualified for "most likely to succeed" in the Zorah High School senior class. By his early twenties, Samson effectively judged Israel and contained the Philistine threat.

Only one enemy stood between Samson and total victory—*lust*. This chink in the wayward warrior's armor led to the defeat of one who had eluded all of Philistia's army.

Now conquered by compromise, Samson lived his last days as a blinded P.O.W. reduced to public ridicule. In this his weakest moment, the Lord poured His strength through Samson to win an unforgettable victory and vindicate God's cause.

HIS ENEMY: LUST
HIS MISTAKE: BEING MORE INTERESTED IN SELF-SATISFACTION THAN IN GOD'S PLEASURE
HIS RECOVERY: BY PRAYING FOR GOD'S HELP IN THE MIDST OF BROKENNESS OVER HIS SIN

Looking back over my early years as a believer, and especially the time I spent in seminary, I cannot rid my mind of the images of Christians I knew who began serving the Lord with great promise, only to end up pathetically defeated. I remember meetings where young people went forward to consecrate their lives to the cause of world missions or to dedicate themselves to a life of service in the Lord's work. Now many of them are working in meaningless jobs, making no measurable impact for the Lord. Many of those who seemed to be the brightest students, the most gifted leaders, or the most articulate public speakers are no longer in the service of the Lord. Some of them have taken a back seat in church leadership, and others have fallen by the wayside completely.

What happens in such cases? How can a person who begins well become a dismal failure so quickly? What happens to those who join the conflict with enthusiasm and zeal for the Lord, only to fall while fighting into defeat and despair? Samson's story is perhaps the classic example of just that kind of life.

The life of Samson stands as a brilliantly lit and wildly flashing warning sign to anyone who would consider being a servant for the cause of Jesus Christ. From Samson we learn the awesome truth that *potential* and *willingness* alone are not all that God requires for a fruitful ministry. To those who would pursue God's service and whose lives are yet pure, it shouts out the caution, "Let him who thinks he stands take heed lest he fall" (1 Cor. 10:12). To those whose lives are already tainted and blotched with sin, it screams, "Abandon your wayward course and leave that unrighteous path, or you'll find yourself at the end of Samson's path."

All the historical introduction necessary to give us an understanding of Samson's time is summed up in two verses. In Judges 13:1, we read, "Now the sons of Israel again did evil in the sight of the Lord, so that the Lord gave them into the hands of the Philistines forty years." Add to that the theme verse of the Book of Judges: "In those days there was no king in Israel; everyone did what was right in his own eyes" (Jud. 21:25).

By the time we get to the events of Judges 13, Israel is in the throes of the longest period of darkness and oppression of that era. Into that darkness, God is ready to unleash a very bright flash of light in the person of Samson. He was chosen and uniquely endowed by God to subdue the enemy Philistines and to bring the people of God back to a right relationship of true worship. Samson could have been the outstanding chapter in a book that chronicles a bleak and unhappy age, but instead his story unfolds as a clear, simple, and timely warning for every servant of God.

LIMITLESS POTENTIAL

Perhaps no Old Testament character had more raw potential than did Samson. The legacy of his parents was one of faith. He had abilities that put him in a class physically above most men who have ever lived. God Himself had chosen and appointed him to his task as deliverer of the people of God. All this only makes his ultimate defeat more tragic.

A special call. Judges 13:3 tells us of the supernatural events surrounding Samson's birth. An angel appeared to his mother, the wife of a godly man named Manoah, and told her, "Behold now, you are barren and have borne no children, but you shall conceive and give birth to a son." That divine announcement put him in a class with Isaac, John the Baptist, and Christ whose births all were heralded by angels.

A special consecration. Furthermore, Samson was especially consecrated to God for life; God ordained before his birth that he would take a life-long Nazirite's vow. The angel announced, "No razor shall come upon his head, for the boy shall be a Nazirite to God from the womb" (Jud. 13:5). The vow of a Nazirite, described in Numbers 6, was a unique commitment to live a life separated unto God. A number of external symbols of consecration characterized every Nazirite. Three of the most significant ones were that they drank no wine or alcoholic beverages; they would not touch any dead body; and they would not cut their hair.

Normally the period of time during which a man kept his Nazirite vow was up to him. The vow would be for a period of time from about six months to five years or more—it was a matter of individual choice. But for Samson, in view of the special ministry that God wanted to give him, the vow would last a lifetime. He was a unique person, called and ordained by God at a unique time, in a unique way, and for a unique reason.

A special cause. Samson's purpose for being was to deliver Israel from the hands of the Philistines, and he knew it from the beginning. Samson did not face the quandary many of us face in adolescence regarding what to do with our lives. God's angel made it clear to his parents even before his birth: "He shall begin to deliver Israel from the hands of the Philistines" (Jud. 13:5). I can think of no higher calling than to deliver God's people at God's time and in God's way from the hands of their enemy.

A special childhood. Samson was reared in a godly home. Judges 13:8-12 show that his father's heart's desire was to know from the angel of the Lord how he and his wife should train Samson. He implored God to send the angel again to teach them how they should prepare the child. That is a wonderful heritage with which to begin life—godly parents who desire to know the mind of the Lord regarding how their child should be taught.

Special credentials. At first, Samson seemed to be growing and maturing in godliness just as we would expect. Scripture tells us that at the end of his adolescence, "The Lord blessed him" (13:24). Verse 25 tells us that "the Spirit of the Lord began to stir him." When he was about twenty years old, the Spirit of God came upon him in a very special way. That in itself is unusual for Samson's era. Throughout the entire Book of Judges, the Spirit of God is said to have come upon only two other judges—Othniel (chap. 3) and Gideon (chap. 6). In those cases, the Holy Spirit's influence in their lives is mentioned only one time each. But if you read through chapters 13-16, you will see that the Spirit of God came upon Samson on at least five different occasions, with a special endowment of power, authentication, or certification, so that nobody in the land, Jew or Philistine, doubted that Samson was God's man.

Special courage. God endowed Samson with special courage. Judges 15:10-17 tells us that 3,000 men of Judah came to Samson and asked him to let them bind him and turn him over to the Philistines to appease them. Samson agreed to let them tie him up, as long as they promised they wouldn't kill him. So they bound him hand and foot with fresh, strong ropes and delivered him into the hands of the Philistines. Incredibly, he snapped the ropes like thread, picked up the jawbone of an ass, a weapon much smaller than a typical club and not nearly as heavy, and with it he killed a multitude of Philistines.

If there was ever a prime candidate for the ministry, it was Samson. But Samson's life stands as a reminder that where there are great assets in the ministry of God, there is also great accountability. We are stewards of our ministries; we are accountable for that with which God has gifted us. It is required of a steward that he be faithful (1 Cor. 4:2). Potential must be shaped, strengthened, honed, and disciplined by faithful consistency, so that it is translated into daily, holy practice.

LOOSE LIVING

It was at just this point that Samson didn't cut it. He failed at living a consistent life. All of that *limitless potential,* the heritage, abilities, and talents God had given him, were mixed with *loose living.* Little cracks began to form in the dike, and one day the flood waters of lust broke through and destroyed his testimony, his usefulness, and his ministry. How often have you seen that happen in the lives of God's choice servants who let their guards down?

Let me suggest eight reasons Samson fell. Each of them represents a danger we all face as stewards of the things of God. Each one is so subtle, so insidious, so deadly, that any one of them can lead to defeat of even God's strongest warriors, as we see in the life of Samson.

He disregarded his parents. Samson disregarded the wise counsel of his parents. Judges 14:1-4 tells us that Samson went into Philistine territory, and there he discovered a good-looking girl. Like many adolescents, he fell for her on sight. But when he came home and told his parents he was in love with a Philistine girl, they said, "Is there no woman among the daughters of your relatives, or among all our people, that you go to take a wife from the uncircumcised Philistines?" (v. 3)

His parents were right, and Samson knew it. One of the fundamental rules of Hebrew Law was that God's people were not to marry heathen people. Although verse 4 tells us that God had in mind to use Samson's marriage to this girl against the Philistines, God did not condone the marriage.

This incident is the first in a series of events that mark a clear pattern of disregard and disobedience in Samson's life, which ultimately led to his defeat. He never learned how to submit to and obey the God-ordained authority in his life. This stubborn determination to marry a Philistine girl regardless of what his parents said was the beginning of the end for Samson.

No one should even consider entering the Lord's service until he learns the importance of submission to God-ordained authority, beginning in the home, and then at school or at work, and in the government, and wherever else God has put him under authority. This theme reverberates throughout Scripture.

He disobeyed God. More significantly, Samson disobeyed God's instructions. As a Hebrew boy growing up in a family where God was honored, he surely knew and understood God's prohibition against marriage to pagan women. Exodus 34 warned the Israelites that they should not marry outside the faith, lest the heathen mates "play the harlot with their gods, and cause your sons also to play the harlot with their gods" (v. 16).

God knew that a pagan mate was a constant temptation to become immoral, reject the true God, and worship false gods. That is exactly what Samson was entering into. Perhaps he thought he was strong enough to resist, but he was heading toward ultimate tragedy—and this was only the beginning. The ages are strewn with the wreckage of saints just like Samson who began with wonderful potential but lost their ministries because they forsook what God has said about a proper life partner.

He desecrated his vows. Having taken one giant step of disobedience, Samson, finding himself outside the path God intended for him, continued to stumble further away. Remember, he had entered into a lifelong Nazirite vow. He had promised not to cut his hair, touch dead things, or drink strong drink. But soon after he began his ministry, and while he was pursuing the Philistine woman, he was surprised by a lion on the road for Timnah. In an incredible display of physical power, Samson killed the lion on the spot (Jud. 14:5-6).

Later Samson encountered the remains of the lion. Some bees had made a hive in the hollow of the carcass, and Samson reached down into that dead lion, to grab a handful of food. In that moment of craving to satisfy a fleshly lust, he broke his vow. Not only did he touch the dead lion, but he also ate honey that was defiled from its contact with the dead animal. As if that wasn't enough, he made a game of his disobedience.

It happened during Samson's wedding feast, while he was celebrating his wicked marriage to a pagan woman, perhaps even drinking wine (which, of course, would have been a further violation of his Nazirite vow). In the frivolity of the occasion, Samson propounded a riddle: "Out of the eater came something to eat, and out of the strong came something sweet" (14:14). He told the thirty men who were at the wedding party that if they could guess what the riddle meant, he would buy some clothing for them; if they couldn't, they must do the same for him. So they put pressure on his new wife, who really had her own interests at heart instead of Samson's, and she gave them the secret.

Samson found himself owing thirty men new wardrobes. Verse 19 tells us what he did: "The Spirit of the Lord came upon him mightily, and he went down to Ashkelon and killed thirty of them and took their spoil, and gave the changes of clothes to those who told the riddle." Think about that for a moment. To get those men's clothing, he had to defile himself by touching more dead bodies. And so he desecrated his vow all over again.

He destroyed his testimony. Not only was Samson unfaithful to his commitment to God, but a number of times in his sinful trek down the path of shameful disobedience, his uncontrolled rage blinded his sense of righteousness. After the riddle was solved and Samson had obtained the clothes, his father-in-law thought that he was angry with his new wife, so he gave her to another man (Jud. 14:19–15:2). That so infuriated Samson that he took three hundred foxes, tied them together in pairs, lit their tails on fire, and turned them loose in the Philistines' wheat fields to burn down all their grain (15:4-5).

The Philistines were so incensed that they took the father-in-law and the girl and burned them alive. That in turn so enraged

Samson that "he struck them ruthlessly with a great slaughter" (15:8). The whole scene reflects a rather brutal and unsophisticated society.

God had indeed called Samson to deliver Israel from the Philistines, but not with random acts of violence spurred by human wrath. Proverbs 29:22 says, "A hot-tempered man abounds in transgression." Man's wrath does not work God's righteousness.

He dulled his spiritual senses. By this point in his life, Samson gave no indication whatsoever that he was cultivating a personal relationship with the living God. His devotional life, as far as we can tell, was nonexistent; his prayer life was limited to times of critical personal need. As a matter of fact, the only two passages in the entire Book of Judges that even mention Samson's relationship with God are both prayers, and they are striking in their selfish focus.

One is in Judges 15, after Samson has slaughtered a thousand men with the jawbone of an ass. He prays, "Thou hast given this great deliverance by the hand of Thy servant, but now shall I die of thirst and fall into the hands of the uncircumcised?" (15:18) Instead of saying a psalm of praise and a hymn of glory to God for the great things He had done, all Samson could think of was his own fleshly needs. As usual, his primary desire was to *feel* good.

How is your devotional life? How much time do you spend in the Word? Whom do you pray for? What is your worship time like? Do you really desire to share Christ with those around you, or are you coldly indifferent? When your devotion to God wanes, when it lacks that zeal and fervor you had as a new Christian, when your hunger for the Word of God begins to evaporate, and when your time in prayer grows shorter and worship seems boring, when you like to be with the world more than with God's people, view those signs as red lights flashing on the dashboard of your life, warning you that your spiritual senses are growing dull. Get into the Word; take time to pray; and rekindle your desire to know God.

He desired his own glory. Another fault that contributed to Samson's downfall was that he was prone to take the credit himself for what God had really done. He made up a little song to celebrate his victory over a thousand men (15:16):

> With the jawbone of a donkey,
> Heaps upon heaps,
> With the jawbone of a donkey
> I have killed a thousand men.

That sings of a heart of pride. It exalts self and neglects God's glory, and it gives us a real insight into the spirit of Samson. He was so consumed with a desire to exalt himself that he completely neglected God's glory.

He defiled his mind. Another step leading to Samson's fall was his inability to subdue his lust, particularly as it related to women. He went from wanting to marry outside the faith to committing fornication with a harlot (16:1). And as if that weren't enough, he got tied up with Delilah. It appears that she was a Philistine, although the text doesn't specifically tell us (16:4).

Perhaps he married her—we don't know that, either. We know one thing about Samson's relationship with her: he was willing to compromise and forfeit his ministry in order to satisfy himself with her. Ultimately, his relationship with her was the destruction of his relationship with God. Her sole purpose was to urge him to betray his people, his vows, and his God—and ultimately she nagged him into it.

He should have known she was plotting to betray him. She kept pressing him to tell her the secret of his superhuman strength. He began to lie to her, and everything he told her, she told his enemies. Nevertheless, he finally broke down under her nagging and told her that the secret to his strength was his long hair (16:17). That was only partly true; the secret of his strength was really the Lord's power, which he had because of his calling and commitment to God. The key to that was his Nazirite vow, and his uncut hair was the sole remaining element of his vow.

What a tragic thing it is to so defile the mind through lust that we lose sight of God's purposes! Yet that is exactly what happened to Samson. It could happen to any servant of God who lets his mind be defiled with impure thoughts. It happened even to David, a man after God's own heart, when he looked at Bathsheba and lusted. If you want to see the deadly seriousness of sins that begin in the mind, just look at the destruction in the lives of David and Samson.

He disclosed his secrets. Another problem plagued Samson; he could not control his tongue. He told the girl from Timnah the answer to the riddle, and although it caused him all kinds of difficulties, he didn't learn his lesson from it. Even though he had every reason to know that Delilah was plotting to betray him to the Philistines, he still gave her the secret of his strength, and it ultimately caused his demise.

LITTLE FRUIT

Samson's witness was neutralized; his hair was cut, he was chained up, and his eyes were gouged out. The Philistines kept him caged like an animal, but one day they brought him out to be ridiculed. More than 3,000 people were there singing songs to the glory of a dead idol, Dagon, while mocking Samson, and more significantly, the living God of Israel, Jehovah (16:23-24).

Samson must have realized in those dreadful moments that he had given occasion for God to be blasphemed. His service for God appeared to be over, and I'm sure there was no joy in his heart. As he considered his condition, he saw that his life was rapidly moving to a close, and anything he might do for the Lord could only hasten his impending death. Perhaps his life flashed before his eyes in that moment, and maybe he experienced a flood of regrets that his departure from the ministry was nothing like he had envisioned it might be.

Samson, the strong man for twenty years, had now been utterly weakened and humiliated. He called to the Lord, "O Lord God, please remember me and please strengthen me just this time, O God, that I may at once be avenged of the Philistines for my two eyes" (16:28). He braced himself between the two central support columns of the building and pushed them apart with all his might. The building collapsed, instantly killing everyone there, including Samson. In my opinion, this was not suicide. It seems likely that Samson was not praying for his life to be taken; he was praying that God might be vindicated, God's cause might be honored—and

he was willing to sacrifice himself if that was what was needed.
It was his most glorious moment, and that is what makes his life so tragic. The most positive thing Scripture can say at this point is, "The dead whom he killed at his death were more than those whom he killed in his life" (v. 30). It's not much of a legacy for one who had begun with as much potential as Samson had. Despite all his strength, despite all the times the Spirit of God came upon him, the greatest thing that could be said of him was that in his last fleeting moment, incarcerated, blinded, and ridiculed, he had killed a lot of Philistines. It was precious little fruit to come from a life so uniquely blessed by God.

LIFE'S LESSONS

Samson's greatest kingdom contribution lies in the warnings his life leaves behind. His legacy should steer you clear of sin's seduction. If you are already sin's target, then flee from it, or you too will bear little fruit just like the wayward warrior.
  Lesson One. God uses us in spite of our sin. Blessing is never necessarily the mark of strength or purity. The Lord did not work through Samson for so long because of his faithfulness—but rather for God's glory. Samson presumed on God's grace.
  Lesson Two. God is not patient forever with sinful living. There comes a time when God removes us from the action. There is no abiding value in being shelved by God.
  Lesson Three. We reap what we sow. The seeds of sin will one day yield a bumper crop of disappointment and defeat. We choose what to plant in the field of our life. God looks for obedience.
  Lesson Four. With repentance comes forgiveness—but not without consequence. We can be off the scrap heap, but we'll not be like new. There is a price to pay for prolonged disobedience.
  Lesson Five. In our moment of failure or weakness, we can still be the channel for God's greatest strength. It stood true for Samson—it can be true for you.
  Lesson Six. Samson's life shouts to us that if we intend to achieve in accordance with the potential that God has placed in us, we must combine our potential with disciplined living.

SEVEN

HABAKKUK:
God's Man from Missouri

"THE SHOW-ME STATE":this slogan marks the Missouri license tag. The same attitude marked Habakkuk. He could not believe the evil that God seemed to tolerate, so he cried heavenward, "Show me!"

In a moment of desperation, Habakkuk admitted that life was not computing. So he turned to the only reasonable course of action—consulting God. When he returned from his season of prayer, Habakkuk was heard to sing, "Now I see."

These facts give us the gist of Habakkuk's experience.

HIS ENEMY: DOUBT
HIS MISTAKE: FOCUSING TOO LONG ON LIFE WITHOUT THE AID OF DIVINE REVELATION
HIS RECOVERY: PRAYERFULLY SEEKING GOD'S PERSPECTIVE TO REORIENT HIS PERSONAL VIEW OF LIFE

I've read and reread Habakkuk. I've tried to live in the shoes of Habakkuk to understand all that went on in his heart. Habakkuk was the perplexed prophet. He was more confused than he was certain that he knew what God was doing in a very immoral world. In a sense, what God affords to us in Habakkuk is an intimate glimpse into the soul of a godly prophet whose faith tottered on the brink of failure. His faith was about to be eclipsed with doubt because God's ways were far beyond his understanding.

Perhaps you can identify with Habakkuk. Maybe you've questioned God, "Why do You allow evil if You are holy and good?" Maybe you've wondered why the unrighteous live with less trouble in the world than do the righteous. Maybe just once you have wanted to scream heavenward, "God, hurry up! Straighten out this messed up world. Make things right! Thy kingdom come! I'm not sure I can stand it much longer."

If you have, welcome to the club. Habakkuk was a charter member. In his day, moral chaos dominated the world, much as it does today. Habakkuk, the godly man that he was, prayed intently that God would invade human history with His righteousness and clean up the mess—but nothing happened. He prayed and he prayed; finally the weight of his own human impatience grew too heavy and the burden of full-time ministry became unbearable. Habakkuk then looked heavenward and wrestled with God over the issues that still plague our minds today.

By looking carefully at this ancient encounter, you'll discover a contemporary message. Undoubtedly some of you will ask the very same questions Habakkuk asked almost 2,600 years ago.

The time is somewhere near 612 B.C. Habakkuk and Jeremiah labored together as the two prophets of Judah. Daniel and Ezekiel at this time were mere teens, prophets in the making; the Assyrians had just recently been replaced as the dominant world power by Babylon.

THE IMPATIENT PROPHET

Our righteous prophet probably had been reading the headlines in the Jerusalem newspaper or listening to the six o'clock news only to discover that the country was in moral decline. Spiritual decay had infected the fabric of society in Palestine. His soul ached. He was a prophet on behalf of God and he preached a message of righteousness, yet the country seemed to be moving further away from righteousness.

Then Habakkuk did that which expressed his name. *Habakkuk* means "one who embraces or one who wrestles." He reached out and emotionally grappled with God over the circumstances. In Habakkuk we go behind the front door of the prophet's chamber and get a glimpse into a private conversation between the prophet and God.

It begins like this:

> How long, O Lord, will I call for help, and Thou wilt not hear? I cry out to Thee, "Violence!" Yet Thou dost not save. Why dost Thou make me see iniquity, and cause me to look on wickedness? Yes, destruction and violence are before me; strife exists and contention arises. Therefore, the law is ignored and justice is never upheld. For the wicked surround the righteous; therefore, justice comes out perverted. (Hab. 1:2-4)

He was baffled; he was befuddled.

GOD'S FIRST REPLY

God responds to Habakkuk in 1:5-11. In effect God says, "Habakkuk, unless I reveal it to you, you will never guess or believe what I am doing. There will come upon you a fierce people like the world has never known, and they will bring havoc upon Palestine like it has never seen before."

That's exactly what happened. By 586 B.C. the city lay in ashes—the temple gone, the population decimated. The remaining Jews were taken captive to Babylon. God basically said, "I understand your impatience, Habakkuk, but just hang on a minute. I'm answering your prayer, but it's not with a 'yes' right now. I'll choose to reform Judah and bring righteousness to her, not from the inside out, but from the outside in."

THE INDIGNANT PROPHET

We'd love to think Habakkuk was tremendously helped with the message. "Lord, it's fantastic that You'd take time to talk to me and tell me these things. I'm just going to continue ministering and rejoice in all that You do." But that's not what happened. Instead of Habakkuk being helped by this direct response from God, it brings even greater horror to his heart. We find that Habakkuk has moved from being the impatient prophet to the indignant prophet. He is *really* upset with God, and he expresses that anger to God in 1:12-27.

After Habakkuk has been incredibly indignant with God, he backs away and says, "I will stand on my guard post and station myself on the rampart; and I will keep watch to see what He will speak to me, and how I may reply when I am reproved" (2:1). Habakkuk said everything that was in his heart and vented all of his indignation. Now he is saying, "I'd better retrench and give myself some room to move around. So Lord, I'm going to stay right where I am and watch. I'm sure after what I've said I'm going to be reproved, but here I am; I'm on station."

Faithful Habakkuk. Habakkuk had said, "Lord, that's unthinkable. How can a holy God use a totally unrighteous nation like Babylon to correct Your own chosen nation?" I think Habakkuk's reasoning went something like this: if the nature of God who authored history is righteous and the character of history is unrighteous, then those two facts are contradictory. Theologians have wrestled with that paradox for decades. It raises the question, How can a righteous God ordain unrighteousness in the world and still be sovereign? People today are asking those same kinds of questions. Maybe you're asking, "Lord, how can You allow a nuclear holocaust? Don't You know that we're created in Your image? Or what about famine and poverty and violent crime and natural disaster?"

In Jeremiah 22:8-9, God laid His finger on why He was doing this to Judah. "And many nations will pass by this city; and they will say to one another, 'Why has the Lord done this to this great city?' Then they will answer, 'Because they forsook the covenant of the Lord their God and bowed down to other gods and served them.' " Why did God judge Judah with a pagan nation? Judah had prostituted herself. She brought in the gods of Babylon and worshiped them more faithfully than she worshiped the Lord.

Why do bad things happen to good people? Because the good people aren't nearly as good as they think they are. Someone ought to write a book titled, *Why Bad Things Happen to Bad People.* Do you know what the answer is? Because we deserve it, and if it were not for God's mercy, things would even be worse than they are.

Habakkuk's conversation with God was incredible. We ought to be thankful that all of our prayers and conversations with God aren't recorded for public disclosure through the centuries as was his.

GOD'S SECOND REPLY

The Lord answered Habakkuk by telling him that one who is proud and boastful will be judged. God is saying that both Judah and Babylon will be judged (2:2-4). "Behold, as for the proud one, his soul is not right within him" (2:4).

The heart of the entire book lies in the second half of verse 4. It was the Word that pierced to the depth of Habakkuk's heart. It was the Word that turned him around. It was the Word that neutralized his impatience and his indignation. "But the righteous will live by faith" (cf. Rom. 1:17; Gal. 3:11; Heb. 10:37-38). I'm sure Habakkuk was stunned by that. He stood back saying, "I'm righteous because I'm righteous in God. I wear the robes of righteousness that God by His grace has given me." I'm sure that as he contemplated his conversation with God, he was saying to himself, "There is no way that my impatience and my indignation over God's plans to use Babylon to judge Judah mark the life of faith."

All the way from verse 5 to the end of the chapter God says, "Habakkuk, if you missed it when I said, 'They will be held guilty' (1:11), let me expand on that for you." "Furthermore, wine betrays the haughty man, so that he does not stay at home. He enlarges his appetite like Sheol, and he is like death, never satisfied. He also gathers to himself all nations and collects to himself all peoples" (2:5). God is talking about Babylon. Like death they were not satisfied till they captured the whole world—all of the human population.

FIVE WOES FOR BABYLON

So God reasoned with Habakkuk, "Will not all of these take up a taunt-song against him, even mockery and insinuations against him?" (2:6) God gave Babylon five woes. In the first God declares that woe would take up a taunt against Babylon for taking financial advantage of the people they had conquered. Dishonesty would also take up its woe against the Chaldeans (2:9-11). Usury and dishonesty—now comes brutality in 2:12-14. Then comes the fourth of five woes: debauchery (2:15-17). Their usury, dishonesty, brutality, and debauchery will come back to haunt them. Then He says that their idolatry will do the same (2:18-20).

Let me paraphrase God's responses as recorded in chapter 2. "There it is. Usury, dishonesty, brutality, debauchery, and idolatry will all come back, Babylon, to pronounce their woes upon you. And by the way, Habakkuk, don't miss that. I am holy. I am everlasting. I am righteous. And I am just. In the end, all things will be done right. That nation will be held guilty. You, Babylon, are guilty, guilty, guilty! You will be judged, and will pay for your sins. But not before I've used you. Unrighteous Babylon, who had very little revelation about Me, I will use you to severely rebuke My chosen people who have received all sorts of signs, wonders, and miracles. They have joined you in your usury, in your dishonesty, in your brutality, in your debauchery, and in your idolatry." God used unrighteous Babylon as His rod of wrath, His tool of chastening, to rebuke a nation who knew better.

Habakkuk had been impatient; he had been indignant. Each time God responded. That's the wonderful thing about God—He is patient. James writes about that: "If you don't understand the trials that you're in, count it all joy and ask God for wisdom who gives to all men liberally and will never rebuke you for asking" (James 1:2-5, author's paraphrase).

THE INTRANSIGENT PROPHET

Something happened in the heart of Habakkuk as he listened to God's second response. As we come to the last phase of Habakkuk's dialogue with God, we find a wonderful characteristic of the prophet. Habakkuk knew he deserved reproof and God had let him off lightly. So he did the only thing he could do. He worshiped God through prayer. One of the most marvelous prayers in all of the Bible is found here where Habakkuk submitted his heart to God. It is written in a highly emotional, poetic form, which speaks of the warm intensity in the heart of Habakkuk.

Petition. In Habakkuk 3:2 we read, "Lord, I have heard the report about Thee and I fear." I fear You, Habakkuk says, not the world! "O Lord, revive Thy work in the midst of the years, in the midst of the years make it known; in wrath remember mercy." In other words, "Lord, if that's the way You're going to do it, go ahead and do it. Permission granted. I'll stand by and watch, but Lord, I petition You that in the midst of Your wrath You would mix a great mercy. Don't give us all that we deserve. I recognize the fact that Judah has not been all that she should have been or could have been. We really have sinned, and we really do deserve Your wrath. But Lord, I pray on behalf of the people, mix Your wrath with mercy."

Praise. Immediately Habakkuk shifts from the petition to praise (3:3-15). It's a wonderful song. It is music of remembrance focused on God's magnificence, glory, might, and power. Habakkuk basically says, "Lord, You have shaken me to the core, but I do remember back to the days in which You manifest Your magnificence. You showed forth Your might. So, Lord, if I am righteous and the righteous live by faith, I'll live by faith and believe You're going to do that again."

Promise. As Habakkuk continues, he makes a promise. It's the most important part of the book, for he really was perplexed, concerned, confused, and shaken by life. So he climbed into the quiet and privacy of his prayer closet and poured his heart out to God. It was a great battle, but his heart was teachable. He responds, "I heard and my inward parts trembled; at the sound my lips quivered. Decay enters my bones, and in my place I tremble. Because I must wait quietly for the day of distress, for the people to arise who will invade us" (3:16). He finally sings, "Lord, I accept it. I accept the fact that we're a sinful people, and You will judge our sin with a righteous rod of wrath. I just accept it, Lord. I'm afraid—but I accept it."

Now here is Habakkuk's promise to God.

> Though the fig tree should not blossom, and there be no fruit on the vines, though the yield of the olive should fail, and the fields produce no food, though the flock should be cut off from the fold, and there be no cattle in the stalls, yet I will exult in the Lord, I will rejoice in the God of my salvation. The Lord God is my strength, and He has made my feet like hinds' feet, and makes me walk on my high places. (3:17-19)

No doubt many of you have struggled or struggle now with the very things that bothered Habakkuk. I think you can see why it's a book for those who doubt. "Lord, why me? Lord, why even at all?" This book is for those who don't understand, who doubt, and who question God. It touches the tender areas of life. There's nothing distant about Habakkuk. He was real; he was genuine; and he was authentic—just as He was before God.

WRAP UP

We learn some basic things from Habakkuk. I think we learn as much from what Habakkuk didn't do as we learn from what he did do. I note first that he didn't abandon God in the crisis, but rather he sought God for answers. Next, he didn't try to redefine God according to his circumstances, but rather he affirmed in his heart that God was who He claimed to be. Third, he didn't publicly shout out his doubts about God, but rather he expressed them in private prayer to God. There was no gossip on the lips of Habakkuk. He went right to God and asked why.

Fourth, Habakkuk first went to God and not to man. In the emergencies of life he didn't cry, "Where's a pastor?" He said, "Where's God? That's who I need." Then, he didn't chuck reality; he didn't decide to abandon life and go off to the desert to live alone. Rather he squarely faced the realities of life, as tough as they were. Sixth, he didn't get mad at God. Although he got indignant, he didn't get mad. As a matter of fact, as he talked to God, it drove him to worship Him, even in the midst of the circumstances.

Seventh, he didn't indict God, but rather he admitted to God his lack of understanding. Last, he didn't plea bargain with God; he didn't try to coerce God into giving him what he wanted, but rather he came to God and said, "Lord, I want an honest answer. Here are the questions. You tell me how and why."

There are also tremendous personal lessons to learn from Habakkuk's example—to know that just as the righteous could live by faith 2,600 years ago, so can we today. As we walk through the valleys of life, we can say there was at least one other man in history who was there too—Habakkuk. If we will follow his path of prayer, God will bring us to the point where we can say, "I will exult in You, O Lord, and I'll rejoice in Your name, and You the Lord God of Israel will be my strength."

We live in an unsettled and unstable world. At the touch of a button a world power could launch a nuclear attack that would obliterate the world. Our situation is volatile, and it's unpredictable. How should we face it? That's the kind of world Habakkuk lived in. He, like us, trembled and dreaded the thought of what would come.

We need to have great confidence and courage for a number of reasons. First, God is the author of history. In Isaiah 46:10 the Lord says that He planned the end from the beginning. Before the world was created, God had a plan. That plan is under God's absolute, total, sovereign control. It's right on schedule.

Second, at times His methods are unknowable apart from the revelation of God. I think we would agree with Habakkuk, and given a chance, we would do things differently from God's ways. I think I would have gone in and held a revival meeting in Jerusalem—a big tent, a lot of trios, duets, and gospel singing. But God knew better. God had a plan that went far beyond Judah. He looked at life with eternity's view, not with the limits of time. While it might be unknowable apart from revelation, God's plan is always believable because it comes from God who is always true.

Third, although the wicked exist, God exercises eternal supremacy over them. I would suggest that any government, no matter how strong and how powerful, is no more than a puppet in the hands of God. When God pulls the strings, they must move in the direction that God moves them.

Fourth, evil will ultimately self-destruct. Sinful mankind will reap what is sown. That was the message Habakkuk missed in 1:11: "Habakkuk, I will judge them." And then God had to expand on that in almost all of chapter 2. "They are sinful and their sin will come back and pronounce a woe on them for destruction."

Fifth, there is a divine discipline for the righteous when they continue to wallow in sin. That's a great warning to all of those who are right with God because of Jesus Christ. God will not tolerate ongoing, rebellious, willful, wreckless sin in our lives any more than He did with the chosen nation Israel. There will be a point in time when God's patience comes to an end. He will judge with His rod of wrath. At times it can be the most unexpected rod (Heb. 12:1-13).

Sixth, faith in our Redeemer, Rock, and Saviour is at the heart of the Book of Habakkuk (2:4). Faith is the anchor that holds when the winds of wickedness blow and when we are fresh out of answers. Faith will keep us on course and save us from being shipwrecked on the shoals of doubt. That is the very faith in God that held Habakkuk firm.

When you, like Habakkuk, begin to feel impatient and indignant and cry out, "Why, Lord? Why me? Why don't You answer my prayer?" let me suggest that you follow Habakkuk's pattern of uncompromising faith. Petition God's mercy, praise God's character, and promise God that from this day forth you will live by faith. That was the message to Habakkuk 2,600 years ago and through his life it is the message to us twentieth-century show-me saints.

EIGHT

MOSES:
A Successful Failure

HAVE YOU EVER FELT INADEQUATE for a task? Feared failure? Thought perhaps God mistakenly tapped you for a ministry? Or maybe you just flat didn't feel like it? Moses knew about all of this and more.

When God called our eighty-year-old reject to the ministry, Moses tried to skate away on the slippery stuff of excuses. Let's watch God melt the ice of Moses' escape route with the heat of His promises.

Look for these important elements in Moses' life.

HIS ENEMY: A POOR SELF-IMAGE
HIS MISTAKE: MAKING EXCUSES FOR NOT TRUSTING AND SERVING
HIS RECOVERY: STEPPING OUT IN FAITH

In Rome stands Michelangelo's renowned statue of Moses. The story goes that when the great sculptor completed his work, he stepped back to praise it, and so lifelike did it appear that he impulsively struck its knee with his hammer, which chipped out a portion of the knee. He exclaimed in frustration, "Why don't you speak to me?"

To this day, that stone statue has not uttered a word in

response, but God, through the living pen of His Holy Spirit, has painted a portrait of Moses for us in the Word of God. It will speak to our heart to stimulate and encourage. What Michelangelo could not do to Moses, God has done. Moses speaks to us in Exodus 3–4.

Going from the Book of Genesis to the Book of Exodus, we bridge almost 300 years, from the death of Joseph to the birth of Moses in about 1552 B.C. Pharaoh had become frightened by Israel because it had grown and expanded as God had promised Abraham. He decided to wipe the nation out by killing all the newly born male children. Through the faith and fortitude of Moses' mother and the grace of Pharaoh's daughter, Moses was brought into the court of Pharaoh, where he was raised.

In the first forty years of Moses' life, he had risen to a position of prominence. Very strikingly, Moses identified with his brethren (2:11-12). He abandoned all the luxury and power of the throne of Egypt to stand with them. However, the brethren misunderstood. Instead of heralding Moses as their deliverer, they turned against him and publicly announced that he was a murderer. With that, Moses fled (2:13-15).

He fled to Midian and herded sheep for forty long years. We pick up the story in Exodus 3. Moses is now eighty years old. Very spectacularly and suddenly, God enters Moses' life.

Do you remember how Moses had his attention drawn to God? He was out in the desert, and he saw a burning bush (3:1-5). To us that might seem odd, but in the very hot deserts of the Sinai Peninsula, it's not uncommon for a bush to catch fire through spontaneous combustion and be consumed immediately. What was special about this bush was that it didn't burn up. Not only was the bush not consumed, but it spoke with the voice of God Almighty.

I AM A NOBODY

God recognized and announced the crisis that faced the nation of Israel; He desired to commission Moses as their deliverer. Things were bad. They had worsened over the past forty years, and God said to Moses, "Therefore, come now, and I will send you to

Pharaoh, so that you may bring My people, the sons of Israel, out of Egypt" (3:10).

We might expect Moses to respond, "Lord, I knew You were going to do that and I knew I was the man; You've trained me brilliantly, and I tried it 40 years ago. I've learned my lesson, and now I'm ready to go." However, that's not exactly how the scene went.

Moses did not respond to God with, "Here am I, send me," but, "Who am I, that I should go to Pharaoh, and that I should bring the sons of Israel out of Egypt?" (3:11) Can't you just hear God under His breath telling Moses, "Now, tell me something I don't know"? He knew Moses had been out in the desert for forty years. He knew Moses had lost his edge and all the sophistication gained in the court of Pharaoh.

Why did Moses respond that way? I suggest that he thought, "What in the world can God do with a failure? I tried it before and they turned against me. They announced me not as a deliverer but as a murderer. I had to flee for my life. I've been out here for forty years suffering and perspiring; my brethren are not around and the luxury of the palace has been lost. Lord, what in the world could You do with me? I failed."

Or perhaps he appealed like this, "Lord, I'm too old. I'm beyond my prime. I've lost my physical strength and my mind is not as sharp as it used to be." However, Moses perfectly fit God's job description for the task at hand. There was never a better equipped man. Paul tells us why in 1 Corinthians 1:26-31.

> For consider your calling, brethren, that there were not many wise according to the flesh, not many mighty, not many noble; but God has chosen the foolish things of the world to shame the wise, and God has chosen the weak things of the world to shame the things which are strong, and the base things of the world and the despised, God has chosen, the things that are not, that He might nullify the things that are, that no man should boast before God. But by His doing you are in Christ Jesus, who became to us wisdom from God, and righteousness and sanctification, and redemption, that, just as it is written, "Let him who boasts, boast in the Lord."

God responded, "Certainly I will be with you, and this shall be the sign to you that it is I who have sent you: when you have brought the people out of Egypt, you shall worship God at this mountain." He pointed out Mt. Horeb which Moses could see rising about 5,000 feet above the elevated plain on which he was herding the sheep of this father-in-law, Jethro.

Do you know how much of a difference God would make in the life of Moses? Exodus 11:3 says that Moses became a leader who was highly esteemed by both the Egyptians and the Jews. Numbers 12:3 notes that he became a man of deep humility. In the Exodus, we see him as liberator and patriot; at Sinai as lawgiver and priest, and in the wilderness as legislator and pioneer. He was a prophet with no equal in all the history of Israel (Deut. 34:10). He was a song writer of note and wrote a song that has lasted longer than any other song that has ever been written (Ex. 15:1-18). Deuteronomy 18:15 indicates that Moses was the prophetic pattern for the coming of Christ. If all of that was not enough, God wonderfully enshrined Moses in the hall of faith (Hebrews 11:23-29).

God made the difference. Moses said, "Who am I?" God said, "You'll be a man whom I am with." What was true of Moses in tandem with God is true of others. Those words, "I will be with you" encouraged the heart of Joshua (Josh. 1:5). Those were the final words Jesus gave the disciples in Galilee, "Lo, I am with you always, even to the end of the age" (Matt. 28:20). In Hebrews 13:5 God promises you and me, "I will never desert you nor will I ever forsake you."

I AM NOT A THEOLOGIAN

Poor Moses. He ran right into a cul-de-sac trying to weasel out of the work of God. When he could not, he did a 180-degree turn and tried another avenue of escape. We find that Moses' second excuse was, "Lord, I am not a theologian." Watch how he reasons. "Behold, I am going to the sons of Israel, and I shall say to them, 'The God of your fathers has sent me to you.' Now they may say to me, 'What is His name?' What shall I say to them?" (3:13)

God beautifully delivers His answer (3:15). "I am who I am."

That is, "I am eternal, everlasting, unchanging, and the same from before the beginning until after the end. Moses, when you return, tell them you've spoken face to face with the 'I Am,' the Jehovah. Tell them you've been in the presence of the God that doesn't change."

It was the name that Abraham knew, the name that Israel knew, and it's the name that you and I know, for it is used over 7,000 times in the Old Testament. It was the way Jesus responded to the Pharisees, when he said, "Before Abraham was born, I AM" (John 8:58). When the soldiers came to take Christ in the garden He said, "Whom do you seek?" They said, "Jesus, the Nazarene." In the Greek language He uttered one word, the verb "to be"—"I AM." Then the Roman soldiers with all of their might and all of their weapons fell to the ground, because they were in the presence of the living God (John 18:4-6).

The next time you, like Moses, doubt the call of God because you are not a seminary graduate or you have not memorized all the Bible or you think you are not an astute theologian, remember one thing—if God has tapped you on the shoulder, not only will His presence be there, but the very power of His eternal being is yours to use in the way God desires.

God had planned Israel's enslavement in Egypt according to His perfect plan. He was right on track as He put His hand on the shoulder of Moses and said, in effect, "You're My man, and now is the time." We also have a divine pledge in 2 Corinthians 1:20. "For as many as may be the promises of God, in Him they are yes; wherefore also by Him is our Amen to the glory of God through us."

Spurgeon had a real handle on the changelessness of God.

> He remains everlastingly the same. There are no furrows on His eternal brow. No age has palseyed Him; no years have marked Him with the momentos of their flight. . . . The Godhead was the same when He was a babe in the manger, as it was when He stretched the curtains of heaven; it was the same God that hung upon the cross and whose blood flowed down in a purple river, the self-same God that holds the world upon His everlasting shoulders, and bears in His hand

the keys of death and hell. He never has been changed in His essence, not even by His incarnation; He remains everlasting, eternal, the one unchanging God.[1]

What great confidence that must have brought to the heart of Moses before whose eyes the plan of God was opening and before whose heart the Word of God unfolded.

If you're a child of God, you did not become one on a trial basis. It does not depend on whether you like or benefit from Christianity. It's an eternal contract, written by God, given as a gift to those whom He calls to His service.

There is really only one of two things we can do in the Christian life. It's like riding a roller coaster. You can either get in, go up the hill, throw your hands up in the air, and have a wonderful time; you can holler and scream and say it's great, even though you may be scared to death. Or you can grab that bar in front of you, have your knuckles turn white, grit your teeth, and just be miserable. But once that bar is shut, you can't get out of the car. You're in because you're in Christ.

I AM UNCONVINCING

Moses pleads, "Lord, I'm a nobody; I'm not a theologian, and now if that's not enough, what if they will not believe me? Or they might say, 'Moses, the Lord hasn't appeared to you.' What do I do then, God?" (Ex. 4:1) God doesn't scratch His head and say, "Boy, I never thought of that." Rather, He immediately responds in 4:2-9.

> "What is that in your hand?" And he said, "A staff." Then He said, "Throw it on the ground." So he threw it on the ground, and it became a serpent; and Moses fled from it. But the Lord said to Moses, "Stretch out your hand and grasp it by its tail"—so he stretched out his hand and caught it, and it became a staff in his hand—"that they may believe that the Lord, the God of their fathers, the God of Abraham, the God of Isaac, and the God of Jacob, has appeared to you." And the Lord furthermore said to him, "Now put your hand into your bosom." So he put his hand into his bosom, and when he took it

out, behold, his hand was leprous like snow. Then He said, "Put your hand into your bosom again." So he put his hand into his bosom again; and when he took it out of his bosom, behold, it was restored like the rest of his flesh. "And it shall come about that if they will not believe you or heed the witness of the first sign, they may believe the witness of the last sign. But it shall be that if they will not believe even these two signs or heed what you say, then you shall take some water from the Nile and pour it on the dry ground; and the water which you take from the Nile will become blood on the dry ground."

God gave authenticating, miraculous works to messengers who were thrust into very special periods of time. These certified that the message they had was from God. Moses was just such a special messenger; the Exodus was a special occasion. God said to Moses, "I'm going to give you some wonderful powers. They will authenticate your message both to the Jews and to Pharaoh."

The miracle of the staff turned into a serpent would be convincing, wouldn't it? From statues, drawings on the pyramids, and the figure on a Pharaoh's diadem, we have learned that an arched cobra was a sign of great power—almost like the old American flag that depicted a snake with the caption, "Don't tread on me." God equipped Moses with a more powerful cobra than the one on Pharaoh's diadem. It convincingly told Pharaoh, "Here is a man who has been endowed by God."

The leprosy miracle was equally impressive. The ancient world had deep fear of leprosy; there was no cure for the dreaded disease. But Moses could conquer the unconquerable; he could cure the incurable; and he could contaminate the uncontaminated.

To fully appreciate the last sign, we have to understand that the Nile was sacred to the Egyptians. Herodotus, the ancient historian, said that Egypt was the gift of the Nile because in the overflowing of its banks, the fertile silt went out to enrich the land. The god of the underworld, whose name was Osiris, was believed to have lived in the Nile, and the Nile was believed to be his bloodstream. When the Nile turned red, it meant that the power of God had slashed the wrists of Osiris and he was bleeding to death. God had power over the whole pantheon of dead Egyptian deities that were worshiped. "Don't worry about being convincing, Moses. I'll do it. And here's exactly how I will do it."

God doesn't use sign miracles today, but He has made some wonderful provisions for us. We've already seen that we're weak—the only kind of people God calls (1 Cor. 1:27). Paul wrote in 2 Corinthians 12:9, "My grace is sufficient for you, for power is perfected in weakness."

I AM NOT A PREACHER

Moses now rushed on to his fourth excuse. "Please Lord, I have never been eloquent, neither recently nor in time past, nor since Thou has spoken to Thy servant; for I am slow of speech and slow of tongue" (4:10). The Hebrew idiom that is used here is "I am heavy of mouth and I am heavy of tongue." It pictures a person with a 100-pound weight tied around his tongue. That graphic phrase helps us to understand what Moses was trying to say. "Lord, there's no way I could get the message out."

Was everything that Moses said true? Perhaps Moses' mind was fogged by the moment, because Acts 7:22 tells us that Moses was a man who had been well educated and was powerful in both deed and word. In 4:11, God responds to Moses, "Who has made man's mouth? Or who makes him dumb or deaf, or seeing or blind? Is it not I, the Lord?" It is interesting that God focuses on the damage that can be done to our senses. Instead of saying, "Moses, I can polish your tongue," He says, "Who is it that makes men dumb so they can't even speak?" Instead of saying, "Moses, I can repair your hearing aid," He asks, "Who is it that makes men deaf?" And instead of saying, "Moses, I'll give you a pair of glasses so you can see if your eyesight is bad," He questions, "Who is it who can make men see?" The answer to these questions was obvious—it is the Creator, God.

He was telling Moses, "Listen, it's harder for Me to make a seeing man blind than to make a seeing man see. And it's tougher to make a talking man dumb than to make a talking man talk. But I can do it. If I can do it for them, I can do it for you. You've talked in the past, and I'll enable you to talk in the future."

God becomes intense with Moses at this point. "Now, then, go, and I, even I, will be with your mouth, and teach you what you are to say" (4:12). In effect He says, "End this nonsense, Moses. Cut the excuses. Quit the foolishness. I will be with you. I will give you My name, I will empower you so you're convincing, and I will put words in your mouth so you can be My accurate messenger."

I AM REALLY NOT INTERESTED

All four of his excuses had failed, so Moses finally pleaded, "Please, Lord, now send the message by whomever Thou wilt" (4:13). Translated from the Hebrew correctly, it comes out something like this, "Oh, Lord, please send someone else to do it. Anybody but me." That was where Moses' heart really was. I rather suspect that was also behind the four preceding excuses too. "Lord, I can't do it. I don't want to do it and I'm not equipped to do it, so just go find someone else." At this point, God's patience is finally exhausted.

> Then the anger of the Lord burned against Moses, and He said, "Is there not your brother Aaron the Levite? I know that he speaks fluently. And moreover, behold, he is coming out to meet you; when he sees you, he will be glad in his heart. And you are to speak to him and put the words in his mouth; and I, even I, will be with your mouth and his mouth, and I will teach you what you are to do. Moreover, he shall speak for you to the people; and it shall come about that he shall be as a mouth for you, and you shall be as God to him. And you shall take in your hand this staff, with which you shall perform the sign." (Ex. 4:14-17)

God says, "Moses, get in gear, and just do it." You say, "He wouldn't do that to us, would He?" Sure He would: "On the contrary, who are you, O man, who answers back to God? The thing molded will not say to the molder, 'Why did you make me like this,' will it? Or does not the potter have a right over the clay, to make from the same lump one vessel for honorable use and another for common use?" (Rom. 9:20)

God never makes a mistake; He's never wrong. To the excuse, "I'm a nobody," He said, "I promise you My divine presence." To the excuse, "I'm not a theologian," He gave Moses the certainty of His divine pledge to accomplish those things that He had prophesied earlier. To the excuse, "I'm not convincing," God provided a divine promise of power. To the excuse, "I'm not a preacher," God said, "I will work through you by divine performance." And to the excuse, "I'm really not interested," God imposed His rightful divine displeasure on Moses.

SO WHAT?

There are a lot of people with a Moses-like heart in a Moses-like situation. God may have His hand on your shoulder, calling you to do something simple, or even something that's incredibly difficult and beyond imagination. God is able. J. Hudson Taylor, the great missionary to China, said, "All of God's giants have been weak men who counted on one thing and one thing only, and that is God being with them when they went to serve Him." That was true for Moses, and it can also be true for you.

As we look at the life of Moses, there are some significant things we ought to learn. We are reminded of the unchanging sufficiency of God. He is without limit. He's inexhaustible. Whatever we need, God is sufficient to provide in full measure. If you're saying, "Lord, I can't because I don't have...." God is saying, "My dear child, you can, because I am sufficient for the day and I am sufficient to the task."

The life of Moses is also a bold declaration that the Lord God makes the difference between success and failure. That which appears to be success without God will be deemed an absolute failure in eternity. That which is done with the presence of God, while it might be deemed a failure in this life, will be catagorized by God in eternity as a success.

The life of Moses also reminds us that age is no barrier to serving God. There are many Christians who say, "Lord, I'm over the hill; I'm out of my prime. My hair is gray. I'm not in the 'now' generation and there's no way you can use me." Moses is a classic example. When he was forty, he was ready to charge. God put him on the shelf for forty years. Then at age eighty, he started. Age is no barrier to being used significantly by God.

The life of Moses ought also to be a stimulus to those who think they're inadequate to participate. If I took a poll, most of us would say, "Lord, I count myself inadequate, weak, and ill-prepared; maybe you had better choose somebody else." At those times, we can remember Moses and how God worked with Him.

The life of Moses is a great encouragement to those who have been shelved by God in the past. Some of you were accelerating in the things of God. All of a sudden tragic sin entered your life, and God put you on the shelf. You felt worthless before God. That's not true. If you'll repent of your sins and begin to grow again in the things of God, you can indeed be of value to God. Moses, Peter, and John Mark were all on the shelf, but God took them off at the right time for the right task and pressed them into service. If you're there, pray that your life would become so right that God will take you off the shelf and put you in the fight again.

The life of Moses is also an incredibly strong exhortation to those of us who would offer excuses rather than willingly accept the call of God. As Moses learned, excuses don't go far with God.

Why was Moses a successful failure? He succeeded in failing to dissuade God from putting him into service. Above his objections, God still used him. Moses then succeeded, although forty years earlier he had failed when he tried prematurely to become the minister that God could use.

An instructive conversation once took place between a seminary student and a seminary professor. The class was homiletics. After the sermons were preached, they went back into the prof's office, and he evaluated them. One day the professor said to a student who had done a rather commendable job, "The sermon you gave yesterday, my son, was mighty fine. The truth you dealt with was well arranged and well presented. But your sermon had one omission, and it was indeed a grave one. For in it there was no word for a poor sinner like me." God in the life of Moses has provided for us words that encourage and give endurance to poor sinners like you and me.

PART THREE

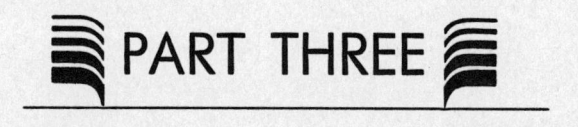

ENCOURAGEMENT: SOME FOUGHT TO VICTORY

NINE

JOSEPH:
God's Valedictorian

DID YOU EVER WANT to steal a glance at your classmate's quiz score to see how he or she did it? God quizzed Joseph on the subject of discipleship. Let's look over his shoulder and peek at the results. You'll find Joseph's corrected exam in Genesis 37–50. Look carefully, because we're enrolled for the course on discipleship too, and we'll have to take God's tests too. Joseph's success can help us.

HIS ENEMY:	CIRCUMSTANCES THAT SEEM TO MOVE HIM AWAY FROM GOD'S PURPOSE FOR HIS LIFE
HIS STRATEGY:	RESTING IN THE CONFIDENCE THAT GOD TESTS IN PREPARATION FOR FUTURE USEFULNESS TO HIM
HIS VICTORY:	LOOKING BACK TO SEE HOW GOD USED CIRCUMSTANCES THOUGHT AT FIRST TO BE BAD

Tough days. We all have them. Some are worse than others. Like the one the hard-hat employee reported when he tried to be helpful. The account actually appeared on a company accident form. Bruised and bandaged, the workman related this experience.

When I got to the building I found that the hurricane had knocked off some bricks around the top. So I rigged up a beam with a pulley at the top of the building and hoisted up a couple barrels full of bricks. When I had fixed the damaged area, there were a lot of bricks left over. Then I went to the bottom and began releasing the line. Unfortunately, the barrel of bricks was much heavier than I was—and before I knew what was happening the barrel started coming down, jerking me up. I decided to hang on since I was too far off the ground by then to jump, and halfway up I met the barrel of bricks coming down fast. I received a hard blow on my shoulder. I then continued to the top, banging my head against the beam and getting my fingers pinched and jammed in the pulley. When the barrel hit the ground hard, it burst its bottom, allowing the bricks to spill out. I was now heavier than the barrel. So I started down again at high speed. Halfway down I met the barrel coming up fast and received severe injuries to my shins. When I hit the ground, I landed on the pile of spilled bricks, getting several painful cuts and deep bruises. At this point I must have lost my presence of mind, because I let go of my grip on the line. The barrel came down fast—giving me another blow on my head and putting me in the hospital. I respectfully request sick leave.

No doubt this thought raced through Joseph's mind more than once.

Graduation brings the familiar strains of Sir Edward Elgar's *Pomp and Circumstance*. It always reminds me of God's valedictorian—Joseph—who exited summa cum laude from the University of Life. His major? Adversity. He had mastered tough times. God's songwriter recounts:

And He called for a famine upon the land; He broke the whole staff of bread. He sent a man before them, Joseph, who was sold as a slave. They afflicted his feet with fetters; He himself was laid in irons, until the time that his word came to pass, the word of the Lord tested him. (Ps. 105:16-19)

What we read is a brilliant balance between incredible tragedy and beautiful triumph brought about by God. For a period of time in Joseph's life, it was one step forward and ten steps back. Can you identify with that?

Several years ago on a very cold winter night our family sat around the dinner table in Columbus, Ohio. We were discussing with our daughter Lee, then eight years old, the marks of a good physician. She said, "Number one, a good doctor gives shots that don't hurt. Secondly, good doctors give medicine that always tastes good. And finally, good doctors give lots of lollipops when you do well."

Shots that don't hurt, prescriptions that taste good, and bundles of lollipops to wash away the bad aftertaste—most of us are looking for that in God's dealings with us. We want God's treatment to be without pain. We want it to taste good and to be pleasing. Day in and day out we crave lollipop strokes.

Psalm 105 tells us how Joseph was groomed from adolescence to age thirty to be the human redeemer of Israel. But first he had to endure a process that hurt, tasted lousy, and for thirteen long years yielded not even one lollipop.

However, it didn't start out all bad for Joseph. If we examine his early years, we discover that Joseph entered life with the proverbial "silver spoon" in his mouth. He was the firstborn of Jacob's favorite wife, Rachel (Gen. 30:22-24). That gave Joseph special prominence in the eyes of his father, so much so that he was especially gifted by Jacob. The robe, normally called "of many colors," was more likely a lengthy robe that went down to his ankles and pointed out Joseph's prominence over his other brothers (Gen. 37:3).

Joseph was especially protected by his father when Jacob was returning from exile and met Esau for the first time in twenty years. Not knowing what Esau would do, he lined up his family in a single-file column. The two maids were in front with their children followed by Leah and her children. Guess who was at the very end in case a disaster erupted? Rachel and Joseph stood at the end of the line, positioned by Jacob at the safest possible place (Gen. 33:2).

Joseph was also the Mr. America type, a very handsome young man (Gen. 39:6). If that wasn't enough, he exhibited moral superiority over his brothers and was able to bring a bad report when a bad report was due. He was used by his father while the other sons monitored the flocks. He went to find his brothers, and they weren't where they were supposed to be (Gen. 37:12-17).

On top of all this, God uniquely revealed Himself to Joseph through the medium of dreams to say, "Joseph, you are special; one day you will be a leader. Your father, your mother, and your brothers will bow down, and they will be servants to you" (Gen. 37:5-10).

That was Joseph's beginning. Not bad! Few of us can identify with Joseph's privileged heritage and life experience.

But at age seventeen, suddenly and cataclysmically the bottom dropped out. The process was absolutely necessary for Joseph to become the man of God's design. There existed no detour for God to transform and purify Joseph from raw material into the kind of strong stuff that Joseph needed to deliver the nation of Israel.

One sage put it this way,

> When God wants to drill a man and thrill a man and skill a man, when God wants to mold a man to play for him the noblest part, when He yearns with all His heart to build so great and bold a man that all the world shall be amazed; then watch God's method, watch His ways, how He ruthlessly perfects them who He's royally elected, how He hammers him and hurts him, making shapes and forms, which only God Himself can understand.

Joseph's saga of testing was written for us, that we might ultimately know the outcome of the process. The bad news is that it's inevitable; there's no way to get out of it. The good news is that God is on the throne, and He'll do it for His glory and for our good.

Joseph is the classic example of one who, for more than days, more than months, even more than a decade, underwent that refining, molding process. Under the head of life's circumstances in God's perfect time and place, Joseph emerged as a disciple who had a distinct and definite purpose in serving God.

Let's turn to Genesis 37. We'll look on as God rapidly thrusts five tests in front of Joseph. See what kind of an answer Joseph's life recorded so that in the end he could be labeled God's valedictorian—a Phi Beta Kappa disciple.

FORSAKEN BY HIS FAMILY

Joseph's brothers saw that their father loved Joseph more than he loved them, so they hated him and gave him the silent treatment. "If that's the way it's gonna be, Joseph, we don't even want to talk to you." Joseph had a dream, and he told them the dream, and they hated him even more. Even his dad rebuked him for the dream and the interpretation Joseph gave to it. Genesis 37:11 records that when it was all over his brothers envied him.

Joseph went to check up on his brothers for Jacob; they weren't where they were supposed to be. In a real sense, they knew they had been caught with their hands in the cookie jar. The only solution in their mind was to get rid of Joseph. And so it says in verse 18, "They plotted against him to put him to death." If it had not been for Reuben's intervention, Joseph would have been slain on the spot. But because of God's providential interest in Joseph, he was merely thrown into a waterless pit, there to languish for a time. Later some Midianite traders passed by on their way to Egypt. His brothers lifted Joseph out of the pit and sold him into slavery in Egypt, hundreds of miles away from home in a country that hated Jews (Gen. 37:25-28). There he would supposedly be a slave for life.

What a childhood! It all started so good. And then one day the bottom fell out, the curtain came down and the presence of God in Joseph's life was apparently no longer there. How did Joseph respond? Patiently. He was patient because he had a promise. He remembered those two dreams.

God was faithful to His Word. Look at Genesis 42:6. Almost twenty years had passed in the life of Joseph from the time he was left in the pit to the time at which we pick up his story. Joseph was ruler over all of the land, and his brothers came and bowed down their faces to the ground. By Genesis 50:18, another twenty years has passed, and the brothers were there again bowing down and telling Joseph, "We're your servants: what can we do for you, our master?" All of this is perfect fulfillment of the promise that God had given Joseph in Genesis 37.

Joseph was not only sustained and comforted by a very specific promise that God had given him, but in the midst of the circumstances, Joseph was sustained by his wonderful response of forgiveness. Genesis 41:51 demonstrates how deeply godliness was embedded in the heart of Joseph.

In Pharaoh's court Joseph had been put second in command. Pharaoh provided a wife for Joseph, and she bore two children. Joseph named the firstborn Manasseh. Joseph said, "For . . . God has made me forget all my trouble and all my father's household." In Hebrew *Manasseh* means "making to forget," which results in forgiveness.

How do you think you would have responded? Your brothers hated you, they plotted against you, they threw you in a pit, they considered murder, and finally they dumped you off for a few sheckles on a caravan that was going to Egypt. That's tough to forget, isn't it? It's even tougher to forgive. Let me suggest that it was the power of God operating in Joseph that enabled him to forgive. Joseph told his brothers, "I am your brother Joseph, whom you sold into Egypt" (Gen. 45:3). Can you hear those guys gulping? They're thinking, "Oh, brother, it's all over. We've had it; this guy will execute us."

Joseph continued, "Do not be grieved or angry with yourselves, because you sold me here; for God sent me before you to preserve life" (45:5). Mark it carefully—it was not his brothers, it was God. You might be saying, "I see it in Joseph, and I really believe God did it, but can He do it again and can He do it today?" Here is one of the most touching stories I've ever read to testify that He can.[1]

It began with a bombing during the Korean war. It left a little girl by the name of Kim blind, and it forced her family to wander from house to house begging for food. Her father was so distraught over being unable to care for the family that he sold his eldest daughter into slavery so he would no longer have to feed her. Then in a moment of great depression, he took his remaining two daughters down to the river and attempted to drown them.

JOSEPH: GOD'S VALEDICTORIAN

One drowned, but Kim was able to float a bit, and her dad ultimately rescued her.

Unable to care for her, several weeks later he dropped her on the doorstep of a World Vision home that cared for the deaf and blind, and four years later young Kim came to America, where she was adopted by a family. In the United States it was discovered that this little blind girl, who had in a real sense been orphaned by the traumas of war and whose father had attempted to kill her, had a very lovely singing voice.

As she grew, she bloomed into the flower that God had designed. She received a Fulbright scholarship to pursue her singing and studied music in Vienna, Austria. She returned to America and she sang throughout our country in churches and evangelistic crusades.

In 1974, after twenty-one years away from Korea, Kim returned to her home and there was lovingly reunited by the mercy and kindness of God with her father who two decades before had attempted to drown her.

FLESHLY LUST

After Joseph arrived in Egypt as a slave, the Midianites sold him to Potiphar (Gen. 39:1). Potiphar was the captain of the bodyguard for Pharaoh, and Joseph was distinguished by the fact that the Lord was with him. Potiphar made him chief of his house.

After a while Potiphar's wife looked with desire at Joseph (39:7). She said, "Come lie with me." That's the first kind word Joseph has had in a long time. It wasn't like that in the pit, nor the caravan. It certainly wasn't like that when he was auctioned off as a slave. What do you think went through his mind? "Who would know?" I'm sure as far as Joseph was concerned, who would care? His whole family had abandoned him. And besides, "Why not? You only go around once in life." How would you answer? Look how Joseph answered.

> But he refused and said to his master's wife, "Behold, with me around, my master does not concern himself with anything in the house, and

he has put all that he owns in my charge. There is no one greater in this house than I, and he has withheld nothing from me except you, because you are his wife. How then could I do this great evil, and sin against God?" (Gen. 39:8-9)

Afterward, when she spoke to Joseph daily, he didn't listen to her (Gen. 39:10). On a very ominous day when Joseph was in the house alone and all the servants were gone, she actually grabbed him and said, "Lie with me." Joseph had his mental and emotional track shoes on and all he could do was flee. He ran—and that's the recommended procedure every time when you're faced with lust. *Flee!* Abandon ship, regardless of what it costs you, even if you die in the process. Some of you are in the midst of that test and know what to do. Some of you have already flunked the exam. But God says, "Flee" (1 Cor. 6:18) and "abstain" (1 Thes. 4:3).

Do you know what would have happened to Joseph had he responded positively to the temptations of Mrs. Potiphar? It would have cost him his life and his discipleship for Almighty God. Do you know what will happen to you and me if we say yes to lust and immorality? The very same thing. There are no exceptions. Disasters will always result. Joseph knew that. He responded well. He fled; he abstained; and God honored him.

You say, "Brother, God has really put him through the paces. What an obstacle course! Maybe I'm not so sure I want to be a disciple. It's tough. There's too much pain and not enough rewards." Well, before the ink on Joseph's answer to the second test question was dry, God gave him another.

FALSE CHARGES

Mrs. Potiphar went to Potiphar and said, "Guess what that Jew tried to do with me." False accusations. So Joseph's master took him, put him into the jail where the king's prisoners were confined (Gen. 39:16-20).

"Behind bars now! I was in a pit, my family tried to get rid of me, I did the right thing, and I fled from immorality, and my reward is jail? God, you've got to be kidding." Those thoughts

JOSEPH: GOD'S VALEDICTORIAN

must have run through Joseph's mind.

Joseph is not the only one who has ever been under the pressure of false accusations. Satan accused Job of serving God for ulterior motives (Job 1). The Judean government accused the Prophet Jeremiah of treason when he told them all the disasters that would befall them at the hand of Babylon (Jer. 37). The Jewish leaders accused Jesus of being Beelzebub—Satan himself (Matt. 10:25). Paul was falsely accused by the Philippian residents of inciting a riot and behaving unlawfully (Acts 16).

Maybe some of you face that same battle right now. People have said things about you that are just untrue. How do you respond? How did Joseph respond? Joseph responded with a clear conscience. When he was in jail, he had an interesting conversation with Pharaoh's butler and baker, who just happened to be in prison with him. He said to them very openly and without shame, "I was in fact kidnapped from the land of the Hebrews, and even here I have done nothing that they should have put me into the dungeon" (Gen. 40:15). We don't hear anything like, "Well, Lord, can we make a deal? I'll give up this, if you'll give up that." Or, "It's unfair. How come?" Or, "Lord, it's just too much, I just can't stand it any longer. You've not fulfilled Your part of the bargain—I resign." Have you ever felt that way? You try to bargain with God, and if that doesn't work, you become angry, frustrated, bitter, and sarcastic.

Did you know it is written in the salvation clause of faith in Christ that you can't resign? It's because you didn't apply for the job. God picked you, God redeemed you, God placed you in the body of Christ, and you're today in God's hands and no one, including yourself, can remove you (John 10:29). The testing process is the way God chooses to shape us and to purify us so that we might reflect the image of God in which we were created.

Let's ask, "What if?" What if Daniel had never been taken forcibly to Babylon? The world would have been robbed of one of its greatest statesmen, and you and I would have missed the privilege of reading one of the most spectacular books in all the Bible. What if Christ had never been crucified? You and I would be dead in our sins and lost for all eternity. What if Paul had never been imprisoned in Rome? You and I would not have in our possession the Books of Philippians, Ephesians, Colossians, and Philemon. What if Martin Luther had never been challenged by the Roman church? The Protestant Reformation might never have taken place. What if John Bunyan had never been incarcerated in Bedford prison? You and I might not have today the greatest Christian classic (apart from the Bible) that has ever been written, *Pilgrim's Progress.*

Do you know what the favorite chorus of those in the refining fire is? It goes like this: "Because He lives, I can face tomorrow. Because He lives, all fear is gone. Because I know He holds the future, life is worth the living just because He lives." Do you know what sustained Joseph? It was the thought of God, the thought that because God lives, He is acting on Joseph's behalf and directing his life where He wants it to go.

FORGOTTEN BY FRIENDS

When Joseph was in jail, Pharaoh's butler and baker came and gave Joseph their dreams, which Joseph interpreted. Joseph added, "Only keep me in mind when it goes well with you, and please do me a kindness by mentioning me to Pharaoh, and get me out of this house" (Gen. 40:14).

The two guys left the prison as Joseph had said, and the baker lost his head, but the butler was restored to service—all as Joseph had predicted. "Yet the chief cupbearer did not remember Joseph, but forgot him" (Gen. 40:23).

"You have got to be kidding!" Joseph might have said. "Eleven years and the butler blew it—my best move to get out of prison." And there he was, forsaken, tempted, falsely accused, and forgotten—even by those to whom he had ministered.

Have you ever been forgotten by anybody? You've done them a good deed, you've stood by their side, and all of a sudden they're no longer there. Remember the hurt? And the tears? I'm sure that's what happened to Joseph. He hurt, and the longer life went on, the fewer solutions there seemed to be left. Then one day God gave him what I believe was the severest test of his life.

FAME AND FORTUNE

One day, through a series of divinely devised events, Joseph was removed from prison and brought into the presence of Pharaoh. Pharaoh said, "What you did for my servants, do for me and interpret my dreams of the corn and the cows." Joseph did it correctly because God gave him the interpretation.

After thirteen years of pain and one disaster after another, Joseph suddenly has an audience with the head of the nation of Egypt. Our first response might be, "Look at me! Look at what I did! I've arrived." Joseph's response, however, was to point Pharaoh to God.

Before he interprets the dreams, Joseph tells Pharaoh that God will give Pharaoh a favorable answer (41:16). He notes twice after hearing the dreams that God has told Pharaoh what He's going to do (41:25, 28). He points out that the repetition of the dreams shows that God will do quickly what He's going to do. Where was Joseph's mind focused? It was on the person of God. Joseph, in spite of temptations to do so, didn't look internally. He looked outward, to the one who had sustained him in his misery.

Joseph had been convinced not only from the dreams God had given him, but also from the disasters of his life and his ultimate deliverance in fulfillment of the dreams. All Joseph could think of was God's glory. He had been strengthened by the tests he had passed, so he didn't crumble under the pressures of pride. Joseph had been so purified by the process that there were no signs of the impurity called "self" as he was honored by Pharaoh. He had been fired in the kiln of circumstances to emerge as a man who was strong enough to carry the load of life that God would place on him to redeem (humanly speaking) the nation of Israel.

Before we conclude, two questions need to be honestly answered.

TWO FINAL QUESTIONS

"Why have exams?" If you have ever taught, you know that the constant cry of students is, "Prof, forget the exam. I know it.

There's no need for it. Don't bother." That's what we would like to tell God. "Cancel the exam, God. I'm ready; just put me in the game." But the Word of God says there is no other plan, there is no other way, there is no other process by which God prepares us to enter the game and do God's pleasure.

How many of you would like to be perfect, entire, complete, whole, lacking nothing? Here's God's answer. "Consider it all joy, my brethren, when you encounter various trials, knowing that the testing of your faith produces endurance. And let endurance have its perfect result, that you may be perfect and complete, lacking in nothing" (James 1:2-4). The only way to get there is through the exams of life.

"What is the secret of passing the exams?" Andrew Bonar, a godly Christian scholar, was ministering in Northfield, Massachusetts. D.L. Moody was in charge of the service. As the service ended, Moody impulsively said to Bonar, "These people would love to know how you've lived the victorious life you just talked about. Tell us all about it, Dr. Bonar." He was a rather shy, retiring man, and he was rather hesitant to say anything. But in a very quiet voice he simply said this, "I don't like to speak about myself. But there is one thing. For fifty years I've had access to the throne of grace."

What was Joseph's secret? Access to the throne of God.

In Genesis 50, Joseph is forty years removed from age seventeen when the trail began. Jacob has died, and Joseph's brothers are deeply afraid Joseph is going to let them have it. They believe he's put on a show for Dad, but now that Dad's gone, it's all over. So they come to Joseph and say, "We are your servants" (Gen. 50:18).

From Joseph's response in verse 19-20 we can draw five lessons. He says, "Do not be afraid, for am I in God's place?" It's God's place to vindicate, and it's God's place to bring restitution in the midst of injustice, not ours. Joseph says, "As for you, you meant evil against me." Actors on the stage of life do not always understand the implications of the individual parts they have in the play. Joseph's brothers meant it for evil, but God had other intentions. He adds, God meant it for good." God is on the throne; He's sovereign. Nothing happens apart from His will. Joseph then goes on to say that God meant it for good "in order to bring about this present result, to preserve many people alive." God knows, and only God knows, the process needed to bring about His purposes.

How can we pass the tests? As did Joseph and Dr. Bonar—by taking advantage of our access to the throne of Almighty God.

TEN

JOB:
A Righteous Victor

SATAN ENGAGED JOB in an unscheduled two-round buffeting bout. The devil's accusation that Job practiced a "health and wealth" theology proved false. Job hit the canvas twice under the crushing hand of Satan's blows. However, Job won the match because he never took the full count when floored by the devil's devious scheme of "materialism."

Here is a bird's-eye view of Job's conflict.

HIS ENEMY: PERSONAL TRAGEDY INVOLVING LOSS OF WEALTH, FAMILY, AND HEALTH
HIS STRATEGY: KEEPING HIS EYES ON GOD
HIS VICTORY: ENDURING THROUGH THE SUFFERING AND PAIN FOR GOD'S GLORY WITHOUT UNDERSTANDING THE "WHY" OF IT ALL

On November 19, 1966, Rabbi Harold Kushner was given the news that his only son, Aaron, would suffer and die from a rare disease that strikes just 1 in 7 million people. His son was only three years old when he was diagnosed as having progeria—the rapid aging disease.

On that day, the Rabbi looked heavenward and asked only one question, "If God exists and if He's minimally fair, let alone loving

JOB: A RIGHTEOUS VICTOR

and forgiving, how could He do this to me and to my innocent child?"

It was eleven years later, in 1977, when Aaron died at age fourteen. Then his father sought even harder for the answer to his question. When he thought he'd found it, he published it in a book entitled *When Bad Things Happen to Good People*.[1]

In that book he concluded that there were three possible answers to the question of why all this had happened in his family. Possibility number one was that in this life, people get what they deserve from God. (That makes God nothing more than a cruel despot.) Or, perhaps God is cruel and allows people to get what they don't deserve. (That reduces our Lord to nothing more than a cosmic sadist.) Or if these are not true, then God is not all-powerful and thus cannot prevent people from getting what they don't deserve. (This explanation makes God nothing more than a consecrated weakling.)

Many centuries ago, a great man in his own time faced a deeper crisis than did Rabbi Kushner and his family. Job's family and wealth were one day completely taken, and close on the heels of that disaster came the loss of Job's physical health. The first two chapters of the Book of Job explain why bad things sometimes happen to good people.

As the Book of Job opens, it gives us Job's credentials and tells us a little bit about his character. He was "blameless, upright, fearing God and turning away from evil" (1:1). He was a righteous man: the character of his lifestyle evidenced the presence of God wherever he walked. He had seven sons and three daughters; he was a family man. His possessions are described in verse 3; he was a businessman, apparently able to take care of large numbers of livestock. Job was also a community leader and a philanthropist, considered one of the greatest men in the east (Job 29:7-13).

Job was also a spiritual leader at home (1:4-5). He was much concerned with the spiritual state of his children, that they would walk with God and bless Him daily. Scripture tells us that he offered "burnt offerings according to the number of them all." Job said, "Perhaps my sons have sinned and cursed God in their hearts."

121

Unbeknownst to Job, mere days later he would become the target of Satan's attack. I suppose that if we did not know of Job's character but only knew all that came upon him, we would never guess that it came on a man whose character was pure and whose life was right.

ROUND ONE: WEALTH

God's Confidence. We discover that it's only through the schemes of Satan that all these disasters occurred. The devil attempted to totally discredit the testimony of God's great servant Job. In Job 1:6-8 we see the confidence God had in Job as He commends Job to Satan as a righteous man. When Satan presented himself to God, God asked him, "Have you considered My servant Job? For there is no one like him on the earth, a blameless and upright man, fearing God and turning away from evil."

Satan's challenge. God knew all about Job and God knows all about you and me—the good things and the bad things. There's no height we can climb, no depth to which we can descend to get away from the ever-present mind and eyes of God. But God's confidence and knowledge did not exempt Job from Satan's challenge. Satan answers the Lord after His great commendation of Job and asks, "Does Job fear God for nothing? Hast Thou not made a hedge about him and his house and all that he has, on every side? Thou hast blessed the work of his hands, and his possessions have increased in the land" (1:9-10). Satan is saying, in effect, "Lord, Job worships You for ulterior motives. It's not because of the worthiness of Your righteous character, Your blamelessness, or Your holiness; rather he worships You for what he can get. His motives are not pure; Job is a hypocrite."

You and I face this danger in our world. Satan used the blessing of God to jump on Job's back and accuse him of sinful thinking and wrong motives. Satan is in the same business today. He is standing before God, accusing the brethren (Rev. 12:10).

God's control. In the midst of Satan's challenge, God wanted to affirm one thing. Notice in verse 12 that God is on the throne. Make no mistake about it. Regardless of what happens in our world, what we read in our newspapers, hear in the evening news, or read in the weekly periodicals, God is in control. Before Satan had any sway in the life of Job, he had to obtain God's permission. Unless God had granted Satan limited access, Satan would not have been able to harm Job, and so it is with us. Satan cannot lay a hand on a child of God until God gives permission. Jesus told Simon Peter, "Simon, Simon, behold, Satan has demanded permission to sift you like wheat; but I have prayed for you, that your faith may not fail; and you, when once you have turned again, strengthen your brothers" (Luke 22:31-32). Men like Job and Peter, who have traveled the valleys of life and walked through unbelievable darkness, have endured pain beyond imagination and emerged at the end of the tunnel to encourage you and me.

God also placed limitations on what Satan could do to Job. I want you to note that righteousness in Christ does not provide immunity to believers from Satan's personal attacks. Righteousness in and of itself will never exempt Christians from the attacks of Satan. As a matter of fact, it could even encourage Satan to make us his target. Job forever stands as an example of this fact.

Also note that material blessings in this life are not necessarily an indication of God's blessing for righteous living. Personal holiness will not necessarily bring material wealth and ease of life as a reward in the here and now for walking in the ways of God. Jesus said that God "causes His sun to rise on the evil and the good, and sends rain on the righteous and the unrighteous" (Matt. 5:45).

A very dangerous movement in America promotes the very thing that Satan says motivated Job. It's called the gospel of the good life or the gospel of prosperity, the theology of middle-class American materialism. It teaches that God wills the prosperity of every one of His children and that for a Christian to be in poverty is to be outside of God's intended will. It's to be living a Satan-defeated life, because we're God's children—the King's kids, as some would put it. We should always go first class. That is, instead of small and second-rate, it should always be the biggest and the best—a Cadillac instead of the Volkswagen; diamonds and all the rest because this brings glory to God.

What a tragic contradiction to the truth of Calvary experienced by the King of kings and the Lord of lords! Instead of wearing a crown of splendor, He was blood-stained by the crown of thorns that dug into His brow. He who should have been robed with all of the robes of righteousness was stripped naked and nailed to a cross.

Wealth was never promised in this life, is never given as a guarantee to believers, and will never be found as evidence that you're walking in the ways of God. The Bible nowhere teaches the "name it and claim it" theology that's sweeping our country.

In her book, *God's Will Is Prosperity*, Gloria Copeland writes, "Isaiah 1:19 says, 'If ye be willing and obedient, ye shall eat the good of the land.' The word willing has become a passive word in our thinking. Actually, in this Scripture it's an action word, it involves a decision—if I said I'm willing to live in divine health, I wouldn't just mean, well, if somebody slaps it on me I'll live in it. No, if I'm willing, I've made up my mind to live that way and I've determined that I will live in divine health—I'm not willing to be sick. If you make up your mind, make a quality decision that you're not willing to live in lack but that you're willing to live in divine prosperity and abundance. That Satan cannot stop. Redemption from the curse of poverty is a part of Jesus' substitution work at Calvary. He paid the price for my prosperity, a heavy price, and I will not scorn any part of His work. I deeply appreciate every benefit that His sacrifice provided for me."[2]

There could be nothing further from the truth. Christ died, not for our poverty, but for our sins. Christ was not made into an eternal checkbook at Calvary; He was made sin that He might die for us (2 Cor. 5:21). A man who had bought into this prosperity theology wrote to the person who had urged him to make some financial decisions, "I did just what you said God wanted me to do. But today I'm more in debt and quite frankly, I hate God." That's what poor theology will do. If we buy it, it will take us away from God rather than bring us to Him, allowing Him to be our Rock and Redeemer in the day when the lights go out and the bottom seems to fall out.

My wife and I received a letter from some dear friends who are

JOB: A RIGHTEOUS VICTOR

missionaries in Irian Jaya. They live in a rather primitive part of that island country. Carl and Karen write,

> Back in September, all the conditions were right. I was coming home a day early because gasoline was short in the country, making it impossible to visit Pangkalan Suka. The rivers were so low that the boat couldn't bring the drums of fuel inland, and a light shower beat me to the river, but that never stopped us before. It did this time. I slipped, striking my arm on the seat of the motorcycle which lifted it above my head in the most unnatural position and presto, a shoulder dislocation. It was so easily done that I thought if we played that picture backwards, it would be back in shape again. But we found it wasn't as easy as all that. After an hour of pain and fruitless effort, we decided that I would have to be taken down river to the city of Ketapang. We arrived around 3:30 A.M. in the morning after about a 15 hour cruise. Its a shame so much of it was in the dark because I managed to stay awake the whole time. Within an hour after arrival I was put back together again, and since there was nobody I knew in that city to give me a lift home, which was 50 miles away, I left that same morning on my own bike. And I'm sure the trip did not add to the healing process, but it was nice to be home again.

This testimony represents the life experience of the saints down through the years—those who have suffered and have been slain for the advance of the kingdom. Quite frankly, wealth and prosperity have rarely been known to be associated with Christianity at all.

Job's conflict. Now let's go back to Job and find out what it was that Satan did to Job to infiltrate his mind and cause him to reverse his life priorities. You will be able to identify a little bit with Job as we pick him up in verse 13. "Now it happened on the day when his sons and his daughters were eating and drinking wine in their oldest brother's house, that a messenger came to Job and said, 'The oxen were plowing and the donkeys feeding beside them, and the Sabeans attacked and took them. They also slew the servants with the edge of the sword, and I alone have escaped to tell you.' " Tragedy struck; messenger number one arrived to say that the oxen and the donkeys and a portion of the servants are gone and he alone had escaped to tell the bad news.

I suppose if we stop here, it would have just been a bad day for Job. But a second messenger appeared on the scene, "While he was still speaking, another also came and said, 'The fire of God fell from heaven and burned up the sheep and the servants and consumed them; and I alone have escaped to tell you'" (1:16).

It's the story of a bad day that got worse. No sooner had the words been uttered from the second messenger's mouth, when a third appeared (1:17). "The Chaldeans formed three bands and made a raid on the camels and took them and slew the servants with the edge of the sword; and I alone have escaped to tell you."

I'm sure if the story stopped, Job somehow could have prevented the momentum of Satan's destructive hand upon his life and he would have been thrilled had the fourth messenger not appeared. Job would have been delighted to merely lose his livestock, a great portion of his livelihood, and his servants; but the bad day became utter tragedy. "While [the third messenger] was still speaking, another also came and said, 'Your sons and your daughters were eating and drinking wine in their oldest brother's house, and behold, a great wind came from across the wilderness and struck the four corners of the house, and it fell on the young people and they died; and I alone have escaped to tell you'" (1:18-19).

Maybe some of you have gone through the tragedy of arriving home, perhaps discovering your home was burned to the ground or had been broken into, destroyed, and all your possessions taken. Or maybe you received that unexpected telephone call late one night that told of a loved one, perhaps even one who was as close as a husband or wife or a child who died.

Job's conquest. Carefully watch Job's response to these painful moments. It says in verse 20, "Then Job arose and tore his robe and shaved his head." He first responded as we would to bad news—with woe, with sadness, and with tears. He was a real person. He was filled with the emotions we have over tragedy. But his next response is to be especially marked. "He fell to the ground and worshiped." What an incredible reaction. When he fell to the ground, he acknowledged outwardly by his posture, "Lord, You're the Master and I am the steward. You own it all, and You've only

JOB: A RIGHTEOUS VICTOR

allowed me to use it."

Then we read these tremendous words, " 'Naked I came from my mother's womb, and naked I shall return there. The Lord gave and the Lord has taken away. Blessed be the name of the Lord.' Through all of this Job did not sin nor did he blame God" (1:21-22). Job knew the truth of Psalm 50:12 where God said, "For the world is Mine, and all it contains." Job refused to yield in the face of Satan's pressure tactics.

C.S. Lewis in his *Screwtape Letters* put these words in the mouth of Uncle Screwtape, "Prosperity knits a man to the world. He feels that he's finding his place in it when really it's finding its place in him. His increasing reputation, his widening circle of acquaintances, his sense of importance, his growing pressure of absorbing an agreeable worth build up in him a sense of being really at home on earth which is just what we want."[3] Those diabolical thoughts that Uncle Screwtape sent to his nephew, Wormwood, are the very thoughts which Satan was attempting to build into the mind of Job. But Job was the victor. It wasn't that Satan's blows missed the mark, for they hit Job exactly where they were aimed. They brought great pain, tragedy, and no doubt questions to his mind; but when it was all over, he bowed down and worshiped. He did not sin with his mouth, nor did he blame God.

Note a couple of things that we learn from Job. One is that Satan attacks even the strongest of believers and the holiest of those that are in Christ. No matter how strong you are or how righteous your lifestyle, you are not immune to the attacks of Satan.

Also, Satan will attempt to discredit your testimony, to cause you to turn your back on God and not only have doubts, but follow them to their logical ends and embrace their devilish conclusions. But be comforted; God allowed and controlled the attack on Job. Job demonstrated that God's confidence in him had been well won.

It's only through the press of life and the trauma of tragedy that who we really are will ever be brought out to be seen by the world. Someone once said, "If you desire to be a skillful mariner, you'll not learn how in a calm sea." We'll never know what's really inside of us until we walk through the valley.

ROUND TWO: HEALTH

There came another day when Satan came before God, and God once again renewed His confidence in Job. He comments on Job's blamelessness, adding, "And he still holds fast his integrity, although you incited Me against him, to ruin him without cause" (2:3).

Satan's relentless challenge. Satan is not at a loss for words. So he responds in effect, "Well, skin for skin, yes, all that a man has he'll give for his life. And Lord, I think quite frankly, Job just relinquished his family and his wealth just to get me off his back, so I won't touch his body. However, put forth thy hand now and touch his bone and his flesh and he will curse Thee to Thy face. God, You touch his body and he'll curse You and turn his back on You and walk in ways that You never imagined" (2:4-5). Satan is suggesting that physical discomfort is always more difficult to handle than material discomfort and more likely to turn us away from a right relationship with God.

God reaffirms His control by allowing Satan to do anything he wants with Job's life without taking it from him (2:6). He must stop short of death. The conditions were clearly spelled out for Satan, and he was obedient to the commands of God. Thus, Job resumes his painful conflict with Satan.

Job's resumed conflict. "Then Satan ... smote Job with sore boils from the sole of his foot to the crown of his head" (2:7). It was not just a minor rash that broke out on his hand, which a little Desinex or Johnson's Baby Powder could have cured overnight. This was the real thing—from the top of his head to the bottom of his soles. He even took a sharp piece of broken pottery and scraped his body with it while he was sitting among the ashes.

It was dismal time for Job, so dismal that throughout the Book of Job we get hints of the severity of his illness. In Job 2:13 it says the pain was so great that when his friends came, they did not speak to him for one whole week, seven days, such a pitiful sight was Job. In Job 3:24 we read that the pain was so great that he groaned at the sight of food and cried tears like gushing torrents of water. Job 7:5 says that there were worms and dirt in his wounds and that fluid ran out all over his body. It was so bad that Job was hallucinating, in and out of complete consciousness, which might explain in part some of the comments made later on (7:14). He was "decaying like a rotten thing" (13:28) and shriveling up (16:8); he suffered from halitosis (19:17) and unrelenting pain (30:17); his skin turned black and his fever raged (30:30); and he experienced dramatic weight loss (33:21). This was Job, a righteous man who did no evil and who had survived the initial onslaught of Satan.

There is a worldwide movement that says there is healing for everyone today. They teach that if you are walking through life with anything but full health, then you're living a faithless life; you're not fully believing the promises of God. But think about it: some of the greatest saints throughout the ages have been sick. Some of the great people in the Bible were sick and died; among them, Isaac, Jacob, and Elisha. Paul was ill; Timothy was ill; Trophimus was ill; Apaphroditus was ill.[4] Everybody that ever lived also died, for Hebrews 9:27 says, "It is appointed unto man once to die, and after this comes judgment." What you do with Christ in the here and now will determine for all eternity whether you live in the wealth of heaven or the poverty of hell.

Job's righteous conquest. If all this were not enough, Satan says, "I've got one more little trick I want to try. Job, if I can't get to you, I'll get to your wife." Up to this point, we've not seen Job's wife. I'm sure she was severely affected by the loss of her children. She took one look at Job and exploded, "Do you still hold fast your integrity? Curse God and die!" (2:9) The very thing that Job had worked so hard to prevent in his children, and the very thing that Satan said would occur, came tumbling forth from the lips of his wife. Satan again wielded his knife, attempting to divide husband and wife. Mrs. Job succumbed to the pressure and pain.

Job carefully handled the circumstances. He had purposed in his heart, no doubt years before, to be a spiritual leader in his family, to be the strength and the sustaining power for both his wife and his children. In the most loving, tender way that he could, he says in verse 10, "You speak as one of the foolish women speaks. Shall we indeed accept good from God and not accept adversity?" She in all likelihood stopped and considered the way of her words. Maybe she responded, "You know, I'm wrong. Thank you for loving me enough to give me those words of chastisement with your deepest love, Job. Draw me back to be your helpmate that we might be the one flesh God intended us to be. Then we won't fall victim to the lies of Satan."

Do you know what Job is saying? God owes us nothing. If adversity comes our way, that's fine; I will still praise God. If blessing comes my way, that's great; I will continue to praise God. Job did not buy Satan's scheme of materialism. He rejected it, and in so doing proved himself a great saint. Satan would have us also believe in materialism today. It thinks like this, "I prize material and physical blessings more highly than my spiritual relationship with Jesus Christ." You say, "Well, I would never think that." I hope you never would, but we'll never know for sure until the ultimate test comes. When we find ourselves in the midst of tragedy, or lose some of our possessions or a portion of our family, or loose our health, then we'll discover our real response to God. Then we will find if our mind has been framed by the Word of God or deceived by Satan.

I wish Rabbi Kushner had read the Book of Job and pondered its message. Had he fully understood the person of God and the wonder of Jesus Christ, he never would have concluded that God is a cruel despot, or that God is a cosmic sadist who brings tragedy upon people even though they didn't deserve it, or that He is a consecrated weakling who could not prevent disaster from coming. Rather he would have discovered, as Job did, that God is a conquering King who rules on His throne.

THE ULTIMATE VICTORY

Turn over to Job 42:5-6. With the tragedies behind, and a four-chapter dialogue with God fresh in his mind (Job 38–41), Job uttered these words. "I have heard of Thee by the hearing of the ear; but now my eye sees Thee; therefore I retract, and I repent in dust and ashes." Job says, in effect, "All the questions I asked and all of those foolish things I said, I take them all back because as You revealed Yourself, Lord, I now see who You are and understand the wonders of Your grace, the brightness of eternal hope and the light that's in Jesus Christ."

This story illustrates so well the life experience of Job—and many of us. An American officer was flying across the ocean alone. Looking out on the horizon, he saw a rapidly approaching storm. He recalled,

> The black inky clouds seemed to be coming on with lightning rapidity. I knew I could not reach shore ahead of the storm. I looked down at the ocean to see if I could go underneath it but the ocean was already boiling over. Knowing that the only thing to do was to rise above it, I turned my frail craft straight up toward the sky and I let her mount and then the storm struck me with all of its fury. It was a hurricane and a cyclone and a typhoon all in one. The sky around me became black as midnight—I could not see a thing. Rain came in torrents and snow began to fly and the hail struck like bullets. But when I climbed to 6,500 feet, suddenly I was swept out into the sunlight and glory such as I never saw in this world before. The clouds were below me, the sapphire sky was bending low above me in amazing splendor, and it seemed the glory of another world. And I immediately began to repeat Scripture to myself and in the heavens above the clouds I worshiped God.

As it was with Job and as it was with the aviator, so it is with us. When the storm comes and life gives us no detour, the only way to go is up. It is only when we've broken through the dark clouds that we will suddenly be introduced to the glory and the splendor of our Holy God who revealed Himself in the person of Jesus Christ. The Saviour shed His precious blood on Calvary so that we sinners, in the midst of life's storms, might find relief.

ELEVEN

RUTH:
God's Cinderella

IN THEIR FAMOUS FAIRY TALES, the brothers Grimm (Ludwig and Wilhelm) tell the tale of Cinderella. This rejected little cinder girl unexpectedly but wonderfully meets a prince who later takes her to be his royal bride.

Ruth was the *original* Cinderella. She was hopelessly lost in pagan Moab, but by God's grace immigrated to Israel. Here she embraced the Lord God, married Boaz, and entered Christ's royal line (Matt. 1:5).

Ruth's remarkable character certifies her as a woman of excellence (Ruth 3:11). She deserves our careful study.

The wonderful account of Ruth's life centers on these basic facts.

HER ENEMY: "WRONG SIDE OF THE TRACKS" BACKGROUND
HER STRATEGY: APPROPRIATING GOD'S GRACE BY IDENTIFYING WITH GOD AND HIS PEOPLE
HER VICTORY: BEING ABLE TO PERPETUATE GOD'S GRACE IN HER FAMILY BY RAISING GODLY CHILDREN WHO IN TURN REPEATED THE CYCLE

RUTH: GOD'S CINDERELLA

Every year *Good Housekeeping* magazine lists the ten most admired women in America. The women chosen are selected for the qualities of courage, compassion, dignity, strength, faith, and integrity. It has been interesting each year to find out who was chosen—and then sometimes to try to figure out why!

In Old Testament time, virtuous women were also honored. Proverbs 31 describes an ideal woman. She is endowed with so many virtues that she seems to us like a superwoman. Twice in Proverbs 31 (vv. 10, 29), the Hebrew word *chayil* (translated "excellent" and "noble" in the *New American Standard Bible*) is used to describe this ideal woman. The word speaks of valor, excellence, attainment, and ultimate virtue. It elevates her to a plane so high that not many women could ever hope to attain to her stature.

Only one woman by name in the Old Testament is said to be *chayil*—Ruth (Ruth 3:11). Interestingly, Ruth was not even a Hebrew; she was a Moabitess. There is value for everyone in looking at what made Ruth such a great woman. She is a model for fathers seeking to build character into the lives of their daughters. She is a pattern for mothers to follow in seeking to be the right kind of woman. She exemplifies for wives the virtues that make a good foundation for marital success. For single women, she sums up the qualities that God seeks to produce in them, and to single men she shows the qualities to look for in a potential mate. For all of us, her life is an example of the best spiritual qualities God desires to be revealed in all His people.

This wonderful woman lived in a not-so-wonderful period of history—the days when the judges governed Israel. That would place her between 1200 and 1020 B.C., 200 years or more after Moses brought the Israelites into the Promised Land. Ruth emerges out of this time as a most unexpected demonstration of the grace and reality of God in the midst of a wicked and perverse generation. She came on the scene in the midst of a tragic and desperate situation.

There was a famine in the land. A man named Elimelech, his wife Naomi, and their two sons left their home in Bethlehem-judah to seek refuge from the famine by living in the land of Moab, about fifty miles away on the other side of the Dead Sea.

Sudden tragedy struck the family. Elimelech died, and Naomi was left with her two sons (Ruth 1:3), who took for themselves Moabite women as wives. One was named Orpah and the other was Ruth. They all lived together in Moab for about ten years, when tragedy struck again, and both of Naomi's sons died (1:5). She was bereaved of her husband and her two children, left as the eldest member of a little family of three widows.

Out of those dire circumstances Ruth emerges as a first-generation believer. Incredibly, she came not from the people of God, but from a pagan nation. Yet because of the new virtues in her life, she graced the lives of all those around her, and thus she shines as an example of what God can do in the life of one who surrenders to Him. At least six virtues in her life stand out as examples to us of what makes a woman excellent. She received them as gifts out of God's hand of grace.

SHE WAS DEVOTED TO HER FAMILY

Perhaps the most immediately visible of Ruth's virtues is that she was devoted to her family. Naomi's husband and then her sons had died. She decided that she would go back to her homeland. She attempted to dissuade Orpah and Ruth from coming with her. Orpah ultimately went back, but Ruth was persistent. Naomi said to Ruth, "Behold, your sister-in-law has gone back to her people and her gods; return after your sister-in-law" (1:15).

Ruth answered, "Do not urge me to leave you or turn back from following you; for where you go, I will go, and where you lodge, I will lodge. Your people shall be my people, and your God, my God. Where you die, I will die, and there will I be buried. Thus may the Lord do to me, and worse, if anything but death parts you and me" (1:16-17).

What a wonderful picture that is of one who is devoted to her family! Proverbs 17:17 says, "A friend loves at all times, and a brother is born for adversity." That describes Ruth's devotion to Naomi, who was the sole remaining tie to her dead husband's family. Having put her commitment to that family in gear, she would not turn back. She had burned her bridges behind her, and she was determined to stay with Naomi.

It is noteworthy that Ruth's commitment to Naomi did not depend on personal gain. She was not following Naomi back to Judah to find money, wealth, or ease of living. Her commitment was to Naomi, even if it brought death. Furthermore, her commitment was so tenacious, so irreversible, that *only* death would ever cancel it.

The sincerity of Ruth's commitment was so evident that Naomi was immediately convinced. When Naomi saw that Ruth was determined to go with her, she said no more (v. 18). Wouldn't you like to have a friend like that? A dear lady a while back gave my wife a little plaque with a saying on it. We hung it in our kitchen so we won't forget it. It says this: "A true friend is one who walks in when the rest of the world walks out."

Maybe you've got a friend like that. They're dear, dear people. Those that you can depend on day in and day out. Hopefully, husbands and wives, that's the way your relationship is. Every man needs a friend like that. Every woman needs a friend like that. And Naomi found a friend like that in Ruth. She had a capacity for deep devotion, total and unswaying commitment.

SHE WAS DILIGENT IN HER WORK

Another of Ruth's virtues is that she was a hard worker. When she and Naomi arrived in Bethlehem, they were widows, living in poverty. Ruth herself was an alien, and Naomi had been gone for years. Furthermore, the harvest season was just beginning, and they had not planted grain.

Ruth asked Naomi for permission to glean grain from the fields (2:2). Despite the adverse circumstances God had placed them in—perhaps *because* of those circumstances—Ruth's eyes were filled only with the great opportunity that lay ahead.

God had made a wonderful provision in the Law for those who found themselves in circumstances like Ruth and Naomi's. "When you reap your harvest in your field and have forgotten a sheaf in the field, you shall not go back to get it; it shall be for the alien, for the orphan, and for the widow, in order that the Lord your God may bless you in all the work of your hands" (Deut. 24:19). God provided for those who had true need, those who through illness, the circumstances of life, or other reasons could not provide for themselves. But they had to work for it. Extra food was left in the field. They could have it if they were willing to come and get it.

Ruth went to the field of Boaz. Ruth 2:1 says that Boaz was a man of great wealth and a relative of Naomi's late husband. In that field, she worked hard. This was the beginning of the barley harvest (1:22), which would have been the last week in April. It would have been very hot, but she gleaned in that field from early in the morning until evening (2:17). Ruth 2:23 tells us that "she stayed close by the maids of Boaz in order to glean until the end of the barley harvest and the wheat harvest." The harvest was seven weeks long, from the end of April to the middle of June. For those weeks she worked from morning to night, from beginning to end. She stuck with her work until it was all over.

Harvest began with Passover at the end of April. It ended with the Feast of Firstfruits, when in an act of worship, God's people would offer Him the firstfruits of the harvest in recognition that it was God who gave the seed, the water, and the sunlight to cause the harvest to grow (Deut. 16:9-12). It was an expression of faith that God would sustain them for a full year. It is an interesting corollary to Ruth's story that because of her faith, her life's account would be recorded in the sacred scrolls that all the Jews would read at the Feast of Firstfruits.

Ironically, Ruth, who embodied everything that a Jew was to be in worship and in work before God Almighty, came from a pagan nation. Perhaps the parallel between Ruth and the woman of Proverbs 31 is most clearly evident in her willingness to work hard (31:14-20, 24, 27). A godly woman does not shrink away from the work that's demanded by life's circumstances.

SHE WAS DEDICATED TO HER GOD

Ruth had a dedication to God that was intense and lasting. This is even more significant in light of her pagan heritage. Ruth, a

Moabitess, was a member of a tribe that had troubled the people of God for years. Moab, you'll remember, was the son born out of an incestuous relationship between Lot and his eldest daughter (Gen. 19:36-37). The Moabites, with the help of the false prophet Balaam, had subverted the Israelites with immorality and idolatry (Num. 22–25). Because of that, the Moabites had been severely judged by God. His judgment was that for ten generations no Moabite could enter the assembly of the Lord (Deut. 23:3).

Nevertheless, before ten generations had passed, God reached into that nation of thorns and clipped a lovely rose in the person of Ruth. She knew her roots, and she may have been aware of God's curse on her people. She knew that she did not deserve the kindness of the Jewish people or the grace of their God, yet she humbly and unreservedly committed her life to Jehovah.

Ruth 2:10 shows just how aware Ruth was of the enmity that existed between the two peoples: "Then she fell on her face, bowing to the ground and said to [Boaz], 'Why have I found favor in your sight that you should take notice of me, since I am a foreigner?'" And again in verse 13, she said, "I have found favor in your sight, my lord, for you have comforted me and indeed have spoken kindly to your maidservant, though I am not like one of your maidservants."

The loveliness of Ruth's character is evident in her humble, dedicated surrender to the will of God. Boaz saw it and answered her, "May the Lord reward your work, and your wages be full from the Lord, the God of Israel, under whose wings you have come to seek refuge" (Ruth 2:12). Ruth, an orphan in an idolatrous land, widowed and left alone in the midst of a dying people who worshiped a lifeless god, sought refuge in the protection of the living God.

Ruth had been schooled in the worship of the pagan god Chemosh. We know a little bit about Chemosh from the other books of Scripture that describe him (Num. 21:29; 1 Kings 11:7; 2 Kings 23:13). He was a god of great violence, to whom, the Moabites and Ammonites would offer their own children as sacrifices. He was a despicable being; everything that holiness is, Chemosh wasn't. Ruth, exposed to the holiness and purity of

Jehovah, totally abandoned Chemosh. She turned her back on him and in repentance turned to the living, loving, Almighty God of Abraham, Isaac, and Jacob. In Him she found salvation and redemption, security and refuge in her darkest moment of need.

Psalm 91:1, 4 declares, "He who dwells in the shelter of the Most High will abide in the shadow of the Almighty. . . . and under His wings you may seek refuge; His faithfulness is a shield and bulwark." Ruth turned to that shield, that under His wings she might find refuge. He rewarded her faith by being a strength for her weakness, a provision for her need, and a fortress to her in what might have been a time of great conflict.

SHE DRESSED WITH CARE

Ruth exemplified 1 Peter 3:3-4: "Let not your adornment be external only—braiding the hair, and wearing gold jewelry, and putting on dresses; but let it be the hidden person of the heart, with the imperishable quality of a gentle and quiet spirit, which is precious in the sight of God." The qualities that made her so attractive are still attractive to us today because God has made them imperishable by declaring them precious in His sight. Hers was an inner beauty that radiated outward. Ruth learned her beauty secrets long before Max Factor and Helena Rubenstein arrived on the scene.

Yet some undoubtedly cry out, "There's no hope for me!" But nothing could be further from the truth. Look at Ezekiel 16:13-14.

> "Thus you were adorned with gold and silver, and your dress was of fine linen, silk, and embroidered cloth. You ate fine flour, honey, and oil; so you were exceedingly beautiful and advanced to royalty. Then your fame went forth among the nations on account of your beauty, for it was perfect because of My splendor which I bestowed on you," declares the Lord God.

According to the prophet, true beauty is allowing yourself to be adorned with the splendor of God. It is available to all, even if you were raised on the wrong side of the tracks. No woman ever needs to consider herself unattractive if she walks with God. That's why Sarah was still "a knockout" to Abraham even when she was ninety.

I highly value this kind of beauty for the women in my life—my mom, my sister, my wife, and my daughter. For her sixteenth birthday I gave my daughter, Lee, a beautiful plaque, on which these words of Tertullian were written in calligraphy.

> Be clothed with the silk of honesty,
> the fine linen of holiness,
> and the purple of chastity:
> thus adorned
> God will be your friend.

That's Ruth's timeless beauty tip to all women for all times.

SHE WAS DISCREET WITH MEN

The loveliness of femininity that begins on the inside works its way out in lifestyle. Ruth displayed her godliness even in her outward attire. We read in chapter 3 that when the harvest season had come to an end and it was time to thresh the grain, Naomi encouraged Ruth to find out if Boaz would like to be her husband. Perhaps she had noticed Boaz had shown supreme favor to Ruth throughout those weeks of harvest.

It is important to understand that the Book of Ruth is not a manual on courtship for the twentieth century. Although Ruth and Boaz's experience might appear strange to us, it was in keeping with the customs of their day. In Ruth 3:3-4, Naomi told Ruth,

> Wash yourself therefore, and anoint yourself and put on your best clothes, and go down to the threshing floor; but do not make yourself known to the man until he has finished eating and drinking. And it shall be when he lies down, that you shall notice the place where he lies, and you shall go and uncover his feet and lie down; then he will tell you what you shall do.

Ruth obeyed. She took her mother-in-law's instructions and put on her best clothes, and went down to the threshing floor to see if Boaz was the man God intended her to spend the remainder of her life with. What happened on the threshing floor that night? That was the holiest night that has ever been spent between two unmarried people. Verse 14 records what happened: "So she lay at his feet until morning and then rose before one could recognize another." They knew God's standard of purity.

You might wonder why Naomi would point Ruth to Boaz. The answer is that he was a member of the family, and it was important that Ruth marry into her dead husband's family in order to perpetuate his family line. This was a common practice in Israel, known as the Levirate marriage. Unmarried male relatives left in the family were to redeem the childless widows. "When brothers live together and one of them dies and has no son, the wife of the deceased shall not be married outside the family to a strange man. Her husband's brother shall go in to her and take her to himself and perform the duty of a husband to her. And it shall be that the first-born whom she bears shall assume the name of his dead brother, that his name may not be blotted out from Israel" (Deut. 25:5-6). That was what was behind Ruth and Naomi's desire to pursue the relationship with Boaz.

The relationship between Ruth and Boaz was pure, holy, and according to the principles set down by God. It was further evidence of Ruth's sincere dedication to the God of Israel.

SHE DELIVERED A BLESSED HERITAGE

Ruth's story ends like a well-crafted romantic novel—only Ruth's story is true. She and Boaz were married, and out of their marriage came a great and wonderful blessing. They had come together, Naomi's family line had been redeemed, a husband had been found for Ruth, and out of that relationship came a son whose name was Obed. Through him Naomi was blessed. Ruth was blessed. Boaz was blessed. Obed no doubt himself was blessed. In fact, through him the whole tribe of Judah—and even the whole world—was blessed.

RUTH: GOD'S CINDERELLA

This little child, you see, was a link in the messianic line. The final verse in Ruth tells us that "to Obed was born Jesse and to Jesse, David," through whom Messiah would come to bless all the world. Not only did Ruth become the great-grandmother of David, but she also found herself thrust directly into the line of the Saviour, Jesus Christ.

Do you see how important Ruth's obedience was to the plan of God? If she had chosen to stay behind in Moab rather than staying with Naomi and following her God, all of biblical history would have been altered. Ultimately, all of Christianity owes a great debt to Ruth's obedience. What a magnificent picture of the grace of God! He took an outcast and orphan Moabite girl, redeemed her, and blessed her obedience by blessing all of humanity through her offspring.

Ruth was the original Cinderella, but her story is not a fairy tale. It is a true account of how God's grace extends to even the lowliest. Ruth went from being hopelessly lost in pagan Moab to being instrumental in the bringing forth of the ultimate Redeemer. Because she embraced the Lord God and married Boaz, she distinguished herself as the great-grandmother of David and thus she entered Christ's royal line.

> What star of Messianic truth
> More beautiful than Gentile Ruth?
> In her the Gentiles find a place
> To share the hope of Judah's race;
> Now see from royal David's line
> One hope for Jew or Gentile shine![1]

TWELVE

DANIEL:
A Man of High Esteem

CHRISTIANS SHARE A COMMON quality with tea bags. Their true contents cannot be known until they've been immersed in hot water. Daniel was plunged into the boiling stuff of adversity more than once.

When his jealous colleagues dunked him for the last time, the best was steeped from Daniel's soul. He emerged loved by the king and highly esteemed by God. His life exuded the taste of "constant character" whose ingredients included integrity (6:1-4); intercession (6:5-10); incessant service (6:16, 20); and indomitable faith (6:23).

Here's an analysis of the battle that Daniel fought.

HIS ENEMY: "SUCCESS AT ANY COST" BUSINESS COLLEAGUES
HIS STRATEGY: IDENTIFYING AND CULTIVATING LIFE QUALITIES HIGHLY VALUED BY GOD AND THEN LIVING THE CONSISTENT CHRISTIAN LIFE
HIS VICTORY: FINDING GOD'S FAVOR EVEN IF IT MEANS EXPERIENCING CAREER OR FINANCIAL LOSS

I hope you have found the study of God's saints a rich experience so far. It's a time to learn; a time to look back in history to see how the Spirit of God has invaded the lives of believers and how God has then used them. We need to look at their lives and pray, "God, use me in the same way."

Some have fallen but later recovered. Anyone who has fallen can have great hope knowing that he is not the first one and that God has been there to pick others up and set them straight.

Some have been endowed with the greatest of spiritual resources; like Solomon or Jonah, but when their ministries were finished, they seemed to be down for the count. They serve a strong warning to those of us who know Jesus Christ. They remind us that daily dependence on God makes the difference whether we win or lose.

BACKGROUND

We look at Daniel, who was a surefire winner. Daniel was a magnificent man. He was a man to whom God revealed more specific prophecy than any man in all of the Bible except John. What difference did knowing the future make in Daniel's life? What kind of impact did God have on Daniel's life as He revealed to him the flow of world history through Babylon, Medo-Persia, Greece, the Roman Empire and then the revived Roman Empire that is yet future (Dan. 7–9)?

Of Daniel we know little outside of the Book of Daniel. He is mentioned once in the New Testament, in Matthew 24:15. There Jesus refers to Daniel 11:31, talking about the abomination of desolation. There is an allusion to Daniel in Hebrews 11:33, "who by faith . . . shut the mouths of lions," referring to Daniel's experience recorded in Daniel 6.

Only twice in the Old Testament, outside of Daniel, is Daniel mentioned. In Ezekiel 28:3 Daniel is marked out as a man of wisdom. In Ezekiel 14:14, 20, Daniel is noted as a man of righteousness. He is named there with Job and Noah—truly a select crowd.

Daniel was a wise man, he was a righteous man, and he was a pure man. Now as we come to the Book of Daniel, we discover that the most noteworthy quality of Daniel is marked out twice. Look with me at Daniel 9 where Daniel is praying. He has been studying the prophecies of the Old Testament and discovered that it was prophecied for Judah to be taken captive to Babylon for seventy years. Daniel notes that those seventy years were about complete, so he begins to pray that God would release the nation and allow them to return home. Gabriel appeared to him in answer to his prayer, calling him "highly esteemed" (Dan. 9:20-24).

Highly esteemed is a marvelous little phrase for us as Christians. It means, You you are *"mega* valuable," you have great worth in the sight and economy of God. In Genesis 27:15 it is used of the choice garments of Esau, the best that he owned. In 2 Chronicles 20:25 it's used of the valuable spoils of war that Jehoshaphat took. In Ezra 8:27 it is used in reference to precious utensils that were used in the tabernacle to offer sacrifices before God. Gabriel was saying in effect "Daniel, you are a man who is highly valued by God. God believes that He can use you greatly."

In 10:10-11 Daniel had another vision, "Behold, a hand touched me and he set me trembling on my hands and knees. And he said to me, 'O Daniel, man of high esteem.' " Then again at 10:18-19, "Then this one with human appearance touched me again and strengthened me. And he said, 'O man of high esteem, do not be afraid.' "

I raise the question, What was it that marked Daniel out in the economy of God and in the language of the angels as a man of high esteem? What is it that was built into the life of Daniel, and what is it that can be developed in your life? What is it that can be cultivated in your daily walk with God that would cause God to look at you and say, "There is a man or woman, there is a teen or collegian of high esteem, one who is incredibly valuable in My economy."

Daniel 6 is one of the most insightful chapters in all of the Bible on godliness. We find there four qualities that mark Daniel out as a man of high esteem. Daniel was dunked in boiling water by his colleagues, but he had been there before. He knew what it was like. When he came out, God said, "Daniel, you are a man of constant character." That was the flavor of Daniel's walk with God.

DANIEL: A MAN OF HIGH ESTEEM

INTEGRITY

We begin by looking at Daniel 6:1-4 where we discover that Daniel was a man marked by integrity, a man who at the end of his life had not faltered. Babylon had been conquered. The king of Daniel 5, Belshazzar, had been defeated by Cyrus, the king of Persia. Darius served in his place. As he began to set up his kingdom, Darius appointed 120 satraps over the kingdom, and over these 120 satraps three commissioners, of whom Daniel was one. These commissioners were to hold the satraps accountable so that the king might not suffer loss (6:2).

Daniel would have been about eighty years old. He began distinguishing himself among the commissioners and satraps because he possessed such an extraordinary spirit (6:3). It was that extraordinary spirit that we discover back when Daniel was a young teen.

I'm impressed to know that what Daniel became as an octogenarian, was what we see in nugget form in Daniel 1. He had been taken captive from his home along with his three friends, Hananiah, Mishael, and Azariah, better known as Shadrach, Meshach, and Abed-nego. Daniel made up his mind as a young person, in a foreign culture, stripped of all the security of home and homeland, not to defile himself with the pagan things of Babylon. As a young teen he had the beginnings of integrity.

In Daniel 6, as a man who had reached his eightieth year, Daniel purposed to continue acting in that mode. He had an extraordinary spirit. It was different, and that special spirit caused him to be noticed by the king. Because that spirit was so obvious, because it was so trustworthy, because it was so righteous, the king planned to appoint Daniel over the entire kingdom. Here is a man who had just served the foreign nation that Medo-Persia had now supplanted, a man whom the Medo-Persians had every reason to suspect. They might have asked, "If he was committed to the Babylonians, what makes us think he will be committed to us, the Medo-Persians, who have just overthrown Babylon?" But Daniel's life was consistent. The testimony of his life had been carried over from one kingdom to the next.

I want you to note that as you live righteously, your life will rebuke unrighteousness. It may produce envy and jealously in those whose righteousness does not match yours. That's exactly what happened to Daniel. The other two commissioners and all 120 satraps began to look for grounds of accusation against Daniel in regard to government affairs (6:4). They were green with envy, raging with jealousy. They wanted to find something wrong with Daniel; they wanted to bring Daniel down to their level.

They could find no ground of accusation, no evidence of corruption, for Daniel was faithful. There was no shoddy statesmanship in the economy of Daniel; there was no dishonest diplomacy. When the audit of Daniel's life was taken, when the books were laid open for internal inspection, his enemies could not find one ground of accusation against Daniel. That's refreshing, isn't it?

As we think of politics in the twentieth century, imagine a politician opening wide his life and having not one ground of accusation found against him. Daniel was truly a man of integrity. Value was found in Daniel's life even by a pagan king, because he knew that in Daniel he had found a man he could trust with the kingdom.

I was recently reading about Admiral Hyman Rickover, father of the nuclear navy.[1] Admiral Rickover was one of a kind. Interviews with potential officers for the nuclear navy were always exciting. They were also frightening, because the one being interviewed never knew what would happen. One young naval officer, a graduate of the Naval Academy who later became President of the United States, Jimmy Carter, sat down in Admiral Rickover's office, and the Admiral asked him what he did best when he was at the Academy. Carter thought about it for a while, and then responded. Rickover put him to the test on those subjects and showed Carter that he didn't know as much as he thought he did.

Then Rickover stopped, looked at Carter and asked him, "Son, tell me something. While you were at the Academy did you do your very best in everything that you did?" Honest man that he was, Carter replied, "Admiral, let me confess that there were those moments in my human weakness that I did not do the best that I could. There were those moments when I did not strive for excellence." Rickover looked at him with eyes that penetrated his soul and asked, "I only have one question. Why? Tell me why on every occasion you did not do your best?"

I find integrity in Daniel of whom it could be asked, "Daniel, on every occasion did you do your best?" Daniel could answer, "I did, for my life was laid open and it was examined by my enemies and they could not find one fault with me."

I commend to you the study of Daniel. It should drive us to become people of integrity. Wherever we are, whatever we do, whether it's at school, a workplace, at a church, wherever it be, we should be like Daniel. We should be people against whom no accusation can be made, people who are incorruptible, faithful, with no negligence found in them.

INTERCESSION

There was a second mark in the life of Daniel. Daniel was an intercessor, a man of habitual prayer. This habit seemed to be the beginning of the end for Daniel. His faithfulness to God in prayer was his apparent downfall.

The other commissioners and the satraps said, "We shall not find any ground of accusation against this Daniel unless we find it against him with regard to the law of his God" (6:5). They came together to the king and spoke to him as follows,

> All the commissioners of the kingdom, the prefects and the satraps, the high officials and the governors have consulted together that the king should establish a statute and enforce an injunction that anyone who makes a petition to any god or man besides you, O king, for thirty days, shall be cast into the lions' den. (6:7)

This was a lie, since Daniel was not a party to this suggestion. They went on to suggest that the king "sign the document so that it may not be changed, according to the law of the Medes and Persians, which may not be revoked" (6:8). Once the law was signed into being, it had to be carried out. Darius signed the document.

What would you do if you were Daniel, knowing that faithfulness to your God in prayer would cause your immediate entrance into the lions' den as a dainty morsel for hungry beasts? Watch how Daniel responded. "Now when Daniel knew that the document was signed he entered his house (now in his roof chamber he had windows open toward Jerusalem); and he continued kneeling on his knees three times a day, praying and giving thanks before his God, as he had been doing previously" (6:10).

Daniel proves to be a man who was an intercessor, a habitual prayer warrior on behalf of the things of God. Daniel distinguished himself as a true spiritual leader. About leaders E.M. Bounds notes,

> They were not leaders because of brilliancy of thought, because they were exhaustless in resources, because of their magnificent culture or native endowment, but because, by the power of prayer, they could command the power of God.[2]

This truth is about to be dramatically demonstrated by Daniel. Daniel was not frightened by that edict. He did not fear the prospect of being thrown to the lions, because he knew one thing—God was a holy God to be feared. He might have asked himself, "Do I want to stand before God and give an answer for why I ceased praying to Him? Or would I rather be fed to the lions and look forward to standing before God and saying, "God, under the most severe accusations and persecution I was able to remain faithful to You."

The satraps and the commissioners had their binoculars out to watch Daniel's every move. These men came by a premeditated plan to pull the rug out from under Daniel. They caught Daniel making petition and supplication before his God.

Do you know what that tells me about Daniel? He was predictable; he was a man of righteous habits. There are those things that need to be regular in our lives. We need to mimic Daniel; so much so that even our worst enemies can point the finger and say, 'I know they'll be praying. I know that on the Lord's Day they go to worship. I know they have regular times to study the Word of God."

When they had seen Daniel praying as they believed that he

would be, they went back and approached the king about the injunction. They threw that statute back in the face of Darius and told him, "Daniel, who is one of the exiles from Judah, pays no attention to you, O king, or to the injunction which you signed, but keeps making his petition three times a day" (6:13).

It's seemingly all over for Daniel. He had violated the law. We would have expected the king to break out in great anger against Daniel: "He's not the man that I thought he was! He's not a man to be trusted with my kingdom." Yet as soon as the king heard this statement, he was "deeply distressed and he set his mind on delivering Daniel" (6:14).

Righteousness in the midst of darkness proved Daniel to be a man who was not only highly valued by God but also highly valued by the king. For the king understood the letter of the law that he had signed, but he also understood its spirit. He understood that Daniel had not violated the spirit of that law, but that at this point Daniel would be judged by its letter.

Daniel's adversaries reminded the king that the law could not be changed or revoked. They had the king over a barrel. The king knew he had been duped. He now understood the motive behind the plot. True to the law, the king gave orders, and Daniel was cast into the lions' den.

INCESSANT SERVICE

Darius had just sentenced the greatest human being in his kingdom to certain death. He came to Daniel and said, "Your God, whom you *constantly serve* will Himself deliver you" (6:16). It was because of Daniel's incessant service, the unbreakable service that he gave to the King of kings, that Darius knew he was a man worthy to serve him and a man worthy of God's miracle to deliver him.

A stone was brought and laid over the mouth of the den, and the king sealed it with his own signet ring and with the signet rings of his nobles so that nothing could be changed in regard to Daniel. Daniel was living on a hope and a prayer at this point. The den had been sealed off; no one could break the seal, and death was imminent. The king went off to his palace, and spent the night fasting. No entertainment was brought before him and he couldn't sleep.

Early in the morning he arose and went quickly to the lions' den to find out what had happened overnight. When he came near to the den he cried out, "Daniel, servant of the living God, has your God, whom you constantly serve, been able to deliver you from the lions?" (6:20)

The king marked Daniel out again as a man of incessant service, a man who sticks with it, a man who endures. Daniel was no 100-yard-dash man in the race of faith; he was a marathoner. He was a man who hit the wall as all marathoners do but refused to quit. When the pain was unbearable, he believed by faith that God would supply whatever he needed.

So it was that Daniel spoke to the king. Daniel had just spent all night with the lions, and he was just as alive and healthy in the morning as he had been the night before. "My God sent His angel and shut the lions' mouths and they have not harmed me, inasmuch as I was found innocent before Him; and also toward you, O king, I have committed no crime" (6:22). Isn't that great? The only government, the only king whom we need to please and serve is God Almighty.

Daniel was noted as a man who continually served his God and, in the midst of crisis, was found innocent by God. He was a man of priorities. He was a man who had undistracted devotion to God. He was a man like Jonathan Edwards, former president of Princeton University in its early days when it was a God-fearing institution. Edwards wrote a diary on a regular basis. One entry notes,

> I claim no right to myself. No right to this understanding, this will, these affections that are in me and neither do I have any right to this body or its members, no right to this tongue, to these hands, feet, ears or eyes, for I have given myself clear away and not retained anything of my own. I've been to God this morning and told Him I've given myself wholly to Him and I've given every power so that for the future I claim no right to myself in any respect. And I've expressly promised Him that by His grace I will not fall. I take Him as my whole portion

and felicity, looking upon nothing else as any part of my happiness. His law is the constant rule of my obedience.[3]

So Jonathan Edwards expressed the heart of Daniel. This is God's desire for our hearts—unceasingly serving God, wholly devoted.

INDOMITABLE FAITH

Not only was Daniel a man of integrity, not only was he an intercessor, not only was he a man of incessant service, but I find that he was also a man of indomitable faith.

The king was delighted when he found Daniel alive, and Daniel was removed from the lions' den unharmed. Daniel's life shouted, "God, in life and in death I'll trust You. Whether the circumstances are good or bad, my faith is in You and it will not be daunted by circumstances. When the odds are against me, I'll believe as much in You as when the odds are for me" (6:23). Daniel was pleasing both to God and to the king.

There's a bit of irony here, for it tells us that after Daniel had been removed from the den, the king gave orders. Those men who had maliciously accused Daniel, their children, and their wives were cast into the lions' den. They had not even reached the bottom of the den before the lions overpowered them and crushed all of their bones (6:24). Note carefully that they were not lions without teeth. They were not lions without appetite. They were not lions who did not have the power to rip Daniel to shreds. Having hungered all night, their mouths closed by the angel of God, they now feasted on those who had slandered Daniel.

GLORIFYING GOD

The end result of Daniel's life was absolutely thrilling, for because of Daniel, "Darius the king wrote to all of the peoples, nations, and men of every language who were living in all the land saying: 'May your peace abound! I make a decree that in all the dominion of my kingdom men are to fear and tremble before the God of Daniel'" (6:25-26). Would you do what Daniel had done if it caused the whole world to hear from the reigning human king that the God of Daniel is the one true living God?

That's what happened. Darius wrote,

> For He is the living God and enduring forever, and His kingdom is one which will not be destroyed, and His dominion will be forever. He delivers and rescues and performs signs and wonders in heaven and on earth, who has also delivered Daniel from the power of the lions.

This victory in the midst of great crisis occurred at the very end of Daniel's life when the tea bag of that octogenarian was dunked in the hottest water he had ever faced. "Constant character" came out of him with a more intense flavor than ever before, so God blessed him in an abundant way and glorified Himself mightily. Look at 6:28: "So this Daniel enjoyed success in the reign of Darius and in the reign of Cyrus the Persian." This capstoned Daniel's life. The fruit of his life was that he enjoyed success. He was a man who satisfactorily accomplished the goal that had been set before him.

Daniel was a man who, as a young teen, purposed in his heart and mind not to defile himself with the sinful practices of a pagan nation. That youthful practice grew, developed, and matured. Daniel was given his ultimate test in the latter years of his life, and he was found true to God. He was honored by the king; he was honored by God.

Can you begin to see why he was highly esteemed by God? Daniel was great because he was a man of integrity, a man of intercession, a man of incessant service, and a man of indomitable faith.

At the heart of Daniel's life pattern rested a passion to glorify God. So it is that Paul exhorts us: "Whether, then, you eat or drink or whatever you do, do all to the glory of God" (1 Cor. 10:31).

NOTES

Foreword

1. H.R. Warfel, *Noah Webster, Schoolmaster to America* (Octagon Press, N.Y., 1966), pp. 181-182.

2. Verna M. Hall & Rosalie J. Slater, *The Bible and the Constitution of the United States of America* (Foundation for American Christian Education, San Francisco, CA, 1983), p. 27.

Introduction

1. David Hubbard, "The Temptation to Quit," in *Hymns for the Family of God* (Paragon Associates Inc.), #615.

Chapter One—Solomon

1. H.C. Leupold, *Exposition of Ecclesiastes* (Baker Book House, 1966), p. 54.

Chapter Two—Jonah

1. J. Sidlow Baxter, *Explore the Book,* Volume 4 (Zondervan Publishing House, 1960), p. 160.

2. *Parade,* August 16, 1981, p. 16.

3. Paul Lee Tan, *Encyclopedia of 7700 Illustrations* (Assurance Pub-

lishers, 1979), p. 1316.

Chapter Three—Eve
1. Robert Silverberg, *Scientists and Scoundrels: A Book of Hoaxes* (Thomas Y. Crowell Co., 1965), p. 234.

2. Jill Morgan, *A Man of the Word* (Baker Book House, 1972).

3. William Ellis, *Billy Sunday* (L.T. Myers, 1914), p. 185.

Chapter Four—Saul
1. Paul Lee Tan, *Encyclopedia of 7700 Illustrations* (Assurance Publishers, 1979), p. 908.

2. *Ibid.,* p. 646.

3. *Ibid.,* p. 910.

Chapter Five—Elijah
1. Charles R. Swindoll, *Three Steps Forward, Two Steps Back* (Thomas Nelson publishers, 1980), p. 19.

2. Charles R. Swindoll, *Killing Giants, Pulling Thorns* (Multnomah Press, 1978), pp. 15-16.

Chapter Eight—Moses
1. Charles Spurgeon, quoted in *Discipleship Journal,* July/August 1981, p. 21

Chapter Nine—Joseph
1. Leslie Flynn, *Joseph: God's Man in Egypt* (Victor Books, 1979), pp. 11-12.

Chapter Ten—Job
1. Harold S. Kushner, *When Bad Things Happen to Good People*

NOTES

(Avon Books, 1981).

2. Quoted in *Eternity,* February 1981, pp. 25-26.

3. C.S. Lewis, *The Best of C.S.* (Christianity Today, Inc., 1969), p. 57.

4. See Richard Mayhue, *Divine Healing Today* (Moody Press, 1983) for a full discussion of sickness, death, and healing.

Chapter Eleven—Ruth
1. J. Sidlow Baxter, *Explore the Book,* Volume Two (Zondervan Publishing House, 1960), p. 31.

Chapter Twelve—Daniel
1. Gordon MacDonald, *Ordering Your Private World* (Moody Press, 1984), pp. 103-104.

2. Quoted by J. Oswald Sanders, *Spiritual Leadership* (Moody Press, 1967) p. 84.

3. Paul Lee Tan, *Encyclopedia of 7700 Illustrations* (Assurance Publishers, 1979), pp. 270-271.